Reincai

Understand Karma, Old Souls and Past Life Experiences

(Perform Spiritual Practices For Nirvana and Heaven)

Joseph Hanlon

Published By **Jordan Levy**

Joseph Hanlon

Reincarnation: Understand Karma, Old Souls and Past Life Experiences (Perform Spiritual Practices For Nirvana and Heaven)

ISBN   978-1-7780579-6-0

No part of this guidebook shall be reproduced in any form without permission in writing from the publisher except in the case of brief quotations embodied in critical articles or reviews.

Legal & Disclaimer

The information contained in this ebook is not designed to replace or take the place of any form of medicine or professional medical advice. The information in this ebook has been provided for educational & entertainment purposes only.

The information contained in this book has been compiled from sources deemed reliable, and it is accurate to the best of the Author's knowledge; however, the Author cannot guarantee its accuracy and validity and cannot be held liable for any errors or omissions. Changes are periodically made to this book. You must consult your doctor or get professional medical advice before using any of the suggested remedies, techniques, or information in this book.

Upon using the information contained in this book, you agree to hold harmless the Author from and against any damages, costs, and expenses, including any legal fees potentially resulting from the application of any of the information provided by this guide. This disclaimer applies to any damages or injury caused by the use and application, whether directly or

Table of Contents

Chapter 1: The Egyptians

After considering the existence, among the primitive peoples in the past, of the doctrines regarding Reincarnation, as well as its historical existence among the extinct peoples of that past, we find our way to that ancient land full of mystery--the place of the mystics/occultists of old--the land Isis-the home the builders the Pyramids and the people of Sphinx. It doesn't matter whether these people were direct descendents of Atlantis, the destroyed home of Ancient Wisdom. The Sphinx represents this great race. Its closed lips seem to invite the ultimate question, and one has the feeling that there is a whispered response that might reach an ear willing to listen and hear it. As we continue our quest to find the origin of Reincarnation we again face the Egyptian Sphinx.

Although Metempsychosis' prehistoric origins are obvious, many claim that it was founded in Egypt, along the banks of Nile. India rejects this claim, insisting that the doctrine was conceived by the Ganges not the Nile. The Egyptian conception, however, will be treated at this location, among the ancient countries holding the doctrine. In India, the doctrine is not a thing that has been forgotten, but one which has reached its full flower and is sending out subtle odors to all corners of civilized society. We will therefore not consider India's teachings before we get to the actual stage of the history reincarnation. Herodotus, a centuries-old historian, stated that the Egyptians were the ones who first proposed the theory of the human soul being imperishable. It is believed that the soul travels the circle of all the created forms, on land, in water and in air before it enters the next body. This cycle of existence takes place over three thousand years.

The doctrines of Reincarnation are easily discernible but hidden away in the massed of esoteric doctrines derived from the exoteric Egyptian teachings. The inner circle that was composed of Egyptian mystics believed the inner truths and were open to sharing them with the world. However, the teachings were not kept secret and fragments fell from tables and were greedily absorbed by the people. We can see this by looking at the fragments of historical records that have been preserved, engraved on the bricks and graven in the stones. Not only did they accept the doctrine, but Egypt was the true home of the highest occult beliefs. Occultists of all races have taught the doctrines and teachings regarding various "sheaths", and "bodies" of men. They believe that these teachings were fully transmitted in their original purity in Egypt, along with the Pyramids shadow. There were many changes in the philosophical and religious beliefs over their forty-year history. But the fundamental doctrine about

3

Reincarnation was still held by all occultists until the degenerate descendents of the once-mighty races became so powerful that they outnumbered the remnants of the Ancient Doctrine. The Egyptians believed in "Ka", a divine spirit that dwells within man; Ab,"the intellect or the will; Hati,"the vitality, "Tet,"the astral and etheric bodies; and "Xa," the physical body. Other authorities may have created a slightly new arrangement which corresponds to the various "bodies" of man today as recognized by occultists.

The doctrine of Rebirth was taught by the Ancient Chaldeans. The "Magi", a body of Chaldean mystics occultists and Persian-Chaldean mystics who held the doctrines Reincarnation as a fundamental truth, was also called the Magi. In fact, they were able, through their teachings, to raise the consciousness of the masses at a higher level than Egyptians. The Magi taught the complex nature of the soul and that it could perish from certain parts. Other parts would survive and go on to live through various earth and other-world existences. It then remained pure and was freed from the need for any further incarnations and settled in the realm of ineffable happiness--the region where light is eternal. The teachings also stated that the soul can review all its previous incarnations to see how they relate and gain wisdom. This will aid the soul in its future work helping other races on the earth. The Magi taught that all living entities, organic or otherwise, were only varying manifestations the One Life and Being. Accordingly, the highest knowledge was a feeling of conscious brotherhood, and relationship to all.

Even the Chinese had an esoteric teaching on Reincarnation. It was beneath the outer teachings of the ages. This teaching may be seen in the works of the early philosophers or seers of the race. Especially in the work Lao Tze, a great Chinese sage. Lao-Tze was the mastermind behind the classic "Tao-Teh-King," which teaches Reincarnation to his students and followers. He taught that there was a fundamental principal called "Tao,"which is considered to be identical to the principle of "primordial reason," the manifestation of which was "Teh", or the creative action of the universe. The universe, including his teachings about the human soul, emerged from the union and activity of the Tao and the Teh. It also included the "Tao,"or spiritual principle; as well the "phi,"or semimaterial vital principle that together animate the body. Lao Tze said, "To forget that the true self cannot be destroyed is to live in a state of peril and suffer many tragedies." Know ye, there is a subtle part of man that is spiritual and is the heavenbound portion. That which has anything to do with flesh bones and body, belongs the earth. It is called the Law. Some believe Lao Tze taught that the "huen," after death, would return to the"tao. However, the writings of his early followers show that he truly taught that the human "huen," a person who has lived through many incarnations, could only return to "tao", when it was done with its round of experience. Si Haei states that, "The vital essence, together with the bones, flesh and body, will be dispersed after death." However, the soul (or knowing principle) of the self is preserved and cannot perish. There is no immediate absorption in the Tao of an individuality. It persists and manifests itself as per the Law. Chuang-Tze added that "Death" is not the end of one's life. Teachings from alater, which said that the souls of ancestors abide in the halls and were corrupted, include the teachings about the "kuei" (belly), which perished with the body; the second being the "ling," which was located in the heart or chest. Other Chinese teachers also taught that the soul is made up of three parts. First, the "kuei," which was found in the abdomen, died with the body, while the second, the "ling," which was located in a part of the heart or chest, survived death for some time, but then disintegrated. Third, or "huen," was found in a portion of the brain. This seat survived the disintegration, and went on to other lives.

While it may sound strange to some readers who are not familiar with the topic of Reincarnation, many ancient Druids lived in ancient Gaul and were very familiar with its doctrines. These people, who were often thought of as barbarians, actually had a philosophy based on a high order which later merged into a mystic kind of religion. Many Romans were surprised by the Druids' level and character of philosophical knowledge after they conquered Gallia. Many of them have written records of their experiences, including Aristotle Caesar Lucan Valerius Maximus and Lucan. These facts were also documented by the Christian teachers who succeeded them. See the works St. Clement, St. Cyril (and other early Christian Fathers) for more information. These ancient "barbarians", a group of people who believed in immortality and life, held some of the highest spiritual views of this matter--the mind as well as the soul. Reynaud, who has made these statements after studying the ancient beliefs of this group, says: "If Judea represents in all the world the idea and existence of an absolute God; if Greece or Rome represent the idea and existence of society, Gaul is, as a matter of fact, the idea and existence of immortality. The ancients all admit that nothing described it more. That mysterious folk was regarded as the privileged holder of the secrets and death. The Gauls were a people with an occult philosophy and mystic religion. These beliefs were destroyed by Roman Conquest.

The Druids' philosophy was remarkably similar to the Inner Doctrine of the Egyptians. The traces left by Pythagoreanism or Hermeticism are evident, but the link that held them together is now lost to history. According to legends among the Druids, their order was linked to the ancient Aryan beliefs and teachings. There seems to have been a close connection between these priests (and those of Ancient Greece) as there are stories about offerings being sent to the temples by priests of Gaul. The legend goes that the Druidic tomb, shaped like a monument, was once found on Delphos. It is thought to have been built above the remains of Druid priestesses. Herodotus among others speaks of a secret alliance among the priests of Greece with those of the Druids. Some legends state that Pythagoras was an instructor for the Druidic priests. Also, that Pythagoras was in close contact to the Brahmins of India and the Hermetists. Others claim that Zamolais gave the Druids their first instruction after he was a slave and student under Pythagoras. In any case, it is incredible to see the correspondence between the two schools.

Unfortunately, much of the Druidic teachings is lost. It is therefore difficult to piece together these fragments. The relationship between the Druids with the Pythagorean School and the firm hold of Reincarnation on the Druids is well-established. The Druids taught a spiritual, immaterial part of man called "Awen" which was linked to the Universal Spiritual principle of Life. These fragments are preserved. They said that this "Awen", the animator of all lower forms and life, including animal, vegetable, and mineral, was responsible for the incarnation of man. It was then trapped in the "abysmal circular" state, or "Anufu," where it was held until it was released and allowed to enter the "circleof liberty," called "Abred," which is the human incarnation. This state of Abred encompasses life on all the different planets. Finally, the "Awen," which is the final liberation, passes on to "Circle of Bliss,"or Gwynfid," where he or she resides for a long time in a state of ecstatic Being.

This transcendent state may not be the last. The "Circle of the Infinite,"or the Ceugant, is identical to the union with God of the Persians and Greek Mystics or the Nirvana of the Hindus. It's a sophisticated form of philosophy, but it is not for "barbarians." Particularly when compared against the crude mythology of Roman conquerors.

The Gauls were so well-versed in the practical facets of occultism than they gave every prisoner a five year reprieve after he was sentenced to death. This was in order to help him prepare for a future life by meditation, instruction, or other preparation. Also, this plan prevented any unprepared or guilty soul from being taken into the planes of the departed. All students of occultism who have accepted the teachings about the astral planes are aware of these benefits

The reader will soon understand that the Gauls demonstrated a great deal of progress in spiritual and philosophical matters. It was not due that they were so advanced beyond their neighbors. But rather, it was because they were instructed by Druid Priests. According to legend, the Druidic priests that brought Druid knowledge to Gaul from a far-off country, possibly from Egypt or Greece, is what they were called. We have discussed the connections between their teachings to that of the Pythagoreans. This suggests there was a strong bond between these priests as well the occultists who came from other lands. The Druidic priests were knowledgeable in astrology/astronomy, and the planets played an important role in the teachings. According to some accounts, a large portion of their ritual was influenced by early Jewish rites and worship. Their favorite symbol, mistletoe, was used to symbolize rebirth. The mistletoe signified the new life that is born from the old one. Many traces from the Druids' religious rites can be found in Ancient Britain or Ireland. These folklores include many elements of English folklore.

Many of these traces are based on Irish beliefs about fairies, luck and symbols. Many stories were told about the births of children who were able to recall their former lives. As they grew older, the memory faded. The belief in souls "coming back", however, is a common thread among these people. It is the Druids' inheritance.

Chapter 2: Using Past Life Regression Techniques

While past life regression is often best handled by a hypnotist skilled in this technique, it is not the only method. If you are interested, try the following techniques. If you succeed, then it might be worth moving to a professional.

Self-guided pastlife regression

You can put yourself in the best possible mindset to experience past life regression sessions by setting up your space so that it is dark and cool. Also, a white noise generator might be beneficial.

Relax: Try to relax and think calm thoughts. If you have the space described above, try to calm your mind there. Your mind should be calm but alert. You should also avoid any distractions, such as hunger. Once your mind is relaxed, you should also relax your body. Place yourself in a comfortable sitting or lying position and focus on relaxing the muscles. Begin with your neck. Then, visualize each muscle relaxing individually.

Start by being relaxed. Next, picture a bubble full of white light surrounding yourself. This bubble will be visible in your eye. It will wash over your head and face, neck, arms, neck, shoulders, neck, legs, knees, and feet. This light can be used to protect you from any negative or dangerous effects that self-regression may cause.

Once you're able to visualize the protective aura in your head, start speaking aloud. For five complete breaths, slowly inhale and exhale for five times. The aura should appear brighter each time you take a breath. It will be almost impossible to see it directly. Keep going with this process until you feel totally relaxed and ready.

Get started: You need to locate the deepest and most secure parts of your brain that can recall past life events. Then, with the right mindset, you will be able to enter these parts. Begin by visualizing a long corridor with a single door at the end. While details of the hallway and door aren't crucial, it's worth taking the extra effort to imagine the long hallway with the gate at the beginning in as many details as possible.

The visualization you choose should make you feel that you are actually there. It's best to do something completely different. It doesn't matter what decor you choose, don't let the hallway and doors be confused with anything else. The entrance to your home will always be the one you see.

You will be moving towards the doorway. Now, you should slowly walk down the hallway. Your mind will relax as you go. When you're walking down the hallway, try to keep your eyes on the oldest memories. When you get to the door, remember any specific events from your childhood which led you to believe you might have been able remember past lives.

Walking down the hallway, keep trying to make it as real-life and physical as possible. Think about the scents in the hallway and any other physical sensations. As you get closer, you may start to associate older memories with the doorway. Once your mind is ready to move on to next steps, you will be able to reach the door and grasp the knob.

Like all other things, it is important you provide as much sensory detail to the knob as possible. The more realistic the scenario will be, the more likely the possibility of regression. You can feel the door opening and closing as you slowly and deliberately turn the knob. Once you have opened the door, close them and move through one smooth motion.

Take stock. For those practicing self-pastlife therapy, it is common to rush to the next step and then look at something completely different. This can cause them to lose their concentration and eventually give up. As such, anything you see when you walk through the door must be accepted without reservation as part your past life.

The first thing you should do is focus on what you see. Once that is done, try to keep the memory in your head. One simple color that you first noticed when you walked through the door might turn out to be the blanket your childhood child was wrapped up in. Another vision of leaves could transform into an African safari that you led. The simplest things will stick in your memories the longest. If you really pay attention to the information that your brain provides, you'll be surprised at the amount of information you can recall.

It is important to let the memory details speak for themselves, not to seek them out too actively. An active goal of trying to guide memories with false positives from various artificial sources can lead you to frustration, unproductive disappointment and even more confusion if the memories are not as clear or quick as you expected. Once you're certain you aren't actively guiding past life regression, then you need to trust the information you have received. Because if you take your mind from the memory, even for a moment, it can endanger the connection and cause you o to start over.

If you are having trouble remembering the details beyond the first image, the following exercise will help. To begin, look down and identify the type of shoes that you are wearing in your memory. It will help you ground yourself in the mental space. Even if your shoes are all that is visible, it is enough for you to anchor your mind and give yourself a place from which to start when you return to past life.

You might find yourself in a memory that is especially unpleasant. If you find it difficult or impossible to focus on removing yourself completely from the regression, remember the bright light that surrounds. It is important for you to be focused on this light and to never let anything through the door physically affect you, mentally or physically.

Return to the moment: It can be exhausting and difficult to attain the right mindset to allow past life regression therapy for to be effective. Imagine that your memory is at the end of the hallway, with the door at one end. Now, go towards the door. As you continue walking towards the door keep your eyes on the details. You will soon be able to recall these details when you get up and are ready to start the day.

Do not expect immediate results. You must believe that there is something behind the door. Although past life regression therapy professionals can help you find it, it can be difficult to know if there is. It is important to view remembering past lives as a marathon. Not a sprint. Slow wins the race.

Chapter 3: Recalling Past Lives After Being Reincarnated

Each person has a past life. Take a moment and think about this. Our bodies are kept alive by an undiscovered source of energy. This energy prevents our bodies from decaying. It allows us to think. Feel. Move. Love. Hate. Learn. How is it possible that this energy can be harnessed to allow us to think, feel, move and love? There are so much speculation and theories out there that it is hard to know which one to believe.

One thing's certain: no new souls exist. It's one soul that continues to reincarnate on and off for millions, and even millions, of years. I was informed that an average of 60 million souls live on this planet and that the Creator does no longer create any new souls. Another fact is that out of the 60 billion souls, six and a half million are in the process of incarnation. The soul never dies, only the physical body. Only the soul can find a new vessel.

The reason Past Lives cannot be remembered

All of us have this little bit of knowledge stored in our subconscious. The problem is that most of us don't have enough brains to access such information. Studies have shown that only 10% of brains can be used for freedom, and that memories from past lives are stored somewhere else in the 95% that cannot be used.

This can be considered a blessing in disguise. This allows us a fresh start without having to worry about past events affecting our current lives. These are just a few examples:

1. It is possible that you have done something very wrong in your past life which has hurt many people close to you. You might feel guilty for past acts even though they are no longer part of your life.

2. You recall that you were a wealthy man in your former life. As someone of lower class you'd have to adapt to living modestly.

3. You died when you were in the thirties. Imagine that you suddenly find your spouse in your late eighties or nineties and regain all your memories. What if she recognized your name? Would you still be capable of coming close to her? Can you still act as though nothing ever happened?

It is a good thing that we don't remember our past lives. It protects us against emotional distress and confusion.

Destiny, Reincarnation, Fate

If you are a strong believer and advocate of karma, then this is probably something you heard at some time: "You just can't escape it." But what exactly is destiny, you ask? While most people will claim that destiny is something that has been predetermined for them, it is actually a false assumption.

Destiny doesn't just happen; it is something that is fought for.

Philosophers and theologians alike have devised a formula for destiny throughout history.

Energy is everywhere

It is energy that follows thought.

Belief is based on thought

Reality springs only from belief

Your destiny is determined by your actions.

Although it may seem like our thoughts are powerless, the truth is that they have great power. To overcome the worst thoughts and feelings, we must get rid of them. Negative thoughts cause negative energy which can be transformed into reality. This will allow us to make our destiny. Not because we were created to, but because of what our words and actions have led to.

While we are contemplating the meaning and purpose of our lives, another question may arise. Do all people have a destiny or not? Is there a way to achieve a certain goal without having to use our free will?

The Will of Destiny

Your destiny is theoretically based upon free will. The only problem is that you didn't know what you were doing. Before it can be reincarnated, the soul decides which life it wants. The astral world will help it, but the majority of decisions will be made by you. You'll need to experience love and pain as well as trust, war, hardship, but you will decide how you'll go about it.

But can your fate be changed? Yes and no. Yes and no. It's true that you don't recall what happened, but that doesn't necessarily mean you were not in control of your own destiny. Forcing it to change might make reaching the endgame more difficult. You won't be as able to progress in your consciousness and reach your goals.

It is like fighting yourself to choose a path that is not your destiny. Destiny is a river. The stream flows in a straight line. However, if you move too far from the middle, you'll find it more difficult to follow.

But where does fate enter this equation? Many people believe that fate and destiny can be confused. Your fate is basically your destiny. This is why you should be cautious about your choices during these "destiny moments" as they will impact your entire life.

But how do we know when our destiny moment has arrived. Sometimes destiny will hit you like a fast train. You won't even remember what it was. It's not all science. And it's not like we get a GPS notice saying "Destiny minute right ahead, make a right" every time that we need to take a decision. If your observation skills do not allow you to see the big picture, then perhaps destiny was trying to reach you.

The wind blows on summer days, and destiny is as simple as that. It can send a gentle breeze enough to move you in one direction, but it rarely sends enough power to send you flying toward your destiny. Your reincarnation was intended to help you learn. It is up to you, the listener, to feel the breeze and to see where it goes. Once you are "caught up", you can decide whether you want the moment to end.

Whatever your belief in destiny, it's important to keep your eyes open for things that could impact your life. In 50% of cases you won't recognize it as a moment of destiny until much later when you either realize "that was the best decision I have ever made" or "man, that was stupid." When you make such a decision think about how it will benefit you in the future. If the answer is yes, don't pass up the chance.

Signs that indicate you have been reincarnated

Sometimes we experience strong moments in our past lives, and it continues to influence us in the future. Many believe that what time we lived before this planet has a significant impact on our life experience, personal characteristics and life ability. The more we achieve in life, and the more spiritual experiences we have, the more gifted we will become.

Truth be told, most of us have been reincarnated once in our lives. However, we don't always remember. However, it is believed that your subconscious may become too full of memories and will spill over if you go through the cycle more than once. Here are signs that your most likely been revived:

1. Recurring dreams

Dreams are often a reflection on what's going down in our back minds. A repeated dream is often an indication of trauma or fear. But a repeating dream could also be a reminder of your past.

Many people have stated that they continue to see the same events, visit the same locations or meet the same people repeatedly in dreams. Some people may see towns in the same era as us or even a medieval castle. If this happens and you are able to live with the impression that it is familiar, your soul may have been reincarnated.

2. Deja vu

Perhaps you were doing something new and suddenly felt that you'd done it before. It could have been an important moment in your own life. It's so real that you begin to question your mental health. You wonder if you've ever done something like this before.

Some people claim that the sensation of déjà vu is related to your neurology, while others believe that it's a reflection in a parallel universe. Some believe deja vu is a manifestation of an event in another life. These sensations are often triggered when there is a certain sound, smell, taste, sight or other sensation.

3. Your intuition is very strong

The intuition is basically the ability of tapping into both our unconscious mind and conscious, deep into the springs innate knowledge or primal wisdom. People who have experienced many past lives will automatically have more information to tap into. And the more soul reincarnates you the closer it is to "snatching" that info.

4. You have memories that aren't from this place

It usually happens to children. This often causes parents to panic, wondering "What is wrong with this child?". Technically, they are not lying or imagining things, but they just have the timing wrong. These memories are so accurate, you may still remember them until you become a teenager. After that point you may start questioning yourself about your own sanity.

These memories may simply be caused a misunderstanding or fantasy, an error in your own thoughts, or by something else. However, there is also the possibility that they could be a link to your past lives.

5. Empathic.

Empathic people are capable of feeling and absorbing emotions. Empathic people can sense the feelings of others. Many therapists believe empathic people are just trying to solve their own problems, while focusing their energy towards others. It is possible that empathic people may have gone through multiple incarnations, and reached a point where they are able to host more than just their own problems.

6. Precognition

Do you remember feeling like you knew what was coming up in the near future? Precognition refers to the ability to sense physical sensations and visions. You may call it "quasiscience", however, it is simply proof of a matured spirit that has experienced many cycles of life.

7. Retrocognition

Retrocognition (as you may know) is the exact opposite from precognition. It's the ability, without actual knowledge, to recall specific events from the past. The events can be any of your past lives or objects from the distant.

Retrocognition cannot be proved easily because it's easy to simply google a past event. You might have been through multiple life cycles if this happens.

8. Unexplainable fears and phobias may be a problem.

Your life experiences may leave a permanent mark. These marks can be passed on to your soul and will continue to influence your life. Many people believe that fear is a result of a traumatic event in your past that ended in your death, or left a trace. This could mean that you may have been reincarnated.

9. Certain cultures, time periods, and environments are your favorites

You are a 21st-century resident in an Italian town, but you are attracted to ancient Celtic artifacts, the 19th Century and Asian culture. These attitudes are believed to be remnants of your past lives. It's your soul trying to reconnect to a time when you felt the most happy.

10. You have a feeling of being older than you are.

There are people that are "young at heart," while others feel old even though they're surrounded with older people. These people look like they were born "old souls." However, there is actually a theory that tackles the problem. It is possible to reincarnate a few times and still be a childlike, young-hearted character. However, if your soul has been reincarnated several times, it will mature and you will feel more intelligent than any other person.

Could you relate to these signs for yourself? The more you tried, the more likely it is that you will relate to the signs.

Can Past Lives Still Be Remembered?

Yes, past lives can be remembered if you so desire. Many theories of incarnation originated from people who had an intuitive memory of a past life, even though they weren't spiritually gifted. These pieces were both from children and adults.

However, spiritually advanced people may have psychic ability or intuition. Even if that was not your intention. The speed and strength of this happening to you will depend on who you are as an individual. It depends on your efforts and how you allow them grow. You might discover a wider variety of spiritual abilities by living each life. One such ability is to see into the past.

Have Fun with Past Lives

Most people have shared stories from their lives in the past. You will be amazed at how many of these happened during childhood. It's probably because there is no adult mind saying "no, it's not possible, but I'm imagining." Have you ever wondered why children can see so many things during their early years of life? There are many things you cannot explain. It's because children are more attracted to the spiritual world, which makes it easier for them to remember. However, that doesn't necessarily make them immune from these memories.

These stories were told by members of counseling forums and may either be hilarious or downright creepy. You decide which one.

* First Mother

One woman recalls being little and going to the grocery stores with her mom. She saw a male there. She was a quiet, well-behaved little girl and wouldn't do or say anything that would cause problems. However, her mother was so upset, she had to take the child out of the store.

Her mother saw the child's fear and inquired why she was in such distress as she was sitting in her car. The man that she saw took the girl from her first mom, and she kept her hidden under his floors for several hours. There she fell asleep, and she was then woken up by her new mom. Her biological mother is her mother. It's possible that her "first" mom was her mother in another life.

* Grandmother

Another woman explained to us that her little sister would walk around holding the picture of her grandfather for dear, crying, saying things like "I love you Harvey," and so she could not have known her grandfather. Her mother also revealed that she would always speak things Lucy, her grandmother's grandmother, would have said - even though she didn't know Lucy as well.

* Recurring Visions

One man shared that he suffered from nightmares about drowning and being burned alive ever since he was a child. He could feel the cold, deep water when his body was submerged and could feel his skin burning from being burned. He could always see the faces of others as he was getting burned.

He had dreams that came back over and again, even after he became an adult. He also shared that he felt an emotionally connected to places that were not yet visited or seen.

These are just a few of many stories that we have - there are many others like them - many people recalling their deaths and knowing things they shouldn't have known. To the horror of many parents, these recollections usually occur during childhood's early stages. These recollections show that even though a soul may leave a physical body, it does not stay there for very long.

Exercise Your Knowledge!

* Can we remember our past lives?

* Why is it we can't remember our past lives.

* How can we find the core of our soul?

* How do phobias relate to past lives and other people?

* Is fate and destiny one thing? Why? Why not?

Chapter 4: Materialism

Materialism, the oldest Western philosophical view, is undoubtedly the most important. It's theory for what happens when we die is .... There is absolutely nothing. The moment we die, that is all. Our consciousness arises from the combination of organic and inorganic elements of our nature and ultimately ends at our death. Materialists see all that exists as matter and empty space. Nothing more.

This view originated in Greece just before Socrates. It was popularized by Epicurus in the fourth century BC. Epicurus believed death was the end both of the body and the soul. He should not have been feared. His ancient philosophy has also been a major influence on modern science. He claimed that the events of this world are solely determined by the motion and interactions atoms, which make up the entirety of our being and reality. Democritus is widely considered to be the father and founder of the atomic theory. Widely, he was misunderstood as representing a "Do what the thou wilt" type of lifestyle. He was actually teaching the idea that suffering and pain should be removed from the human's mind, and that the gods should not be fear. He said that after a man dies, he doesn't feel any pain because he no long exists. He said that death is "nothing to us". Fear of dying is caused by the belief that death can bring awareness.

Lucretius was a Roman poet born in the last century of the Christian era. Epicurus inspired his poetry, and he wrote 7400 line philosophical poem De Rerum Natura. His poem is very materialistic because it relies heavily on observation and explanation. Lucretius believed thoughts of a human were a collection of atoms that have been stripped of all other objects in the surrounding environment and then recombined by the brain. Materialists have been describing the world in Rome and

Greece since the beginning based on scientific evidence rather than abstract philosophical reasoning. (scientific proof is in quotations because it is often used to support other philosophical beliefs regarding death). Later, we will explore this concept further.

These materialistic theories were believed to be true even up to the 19thcentury when some believers claimed that thoughts were nothing but atoms moving through space. The men who believed in this theory were all able to agree that it was not empirical scientific. The theory had some metascientific views. One was that nature doesn't have an beginning or an ending, and instead of a supernatural entity keeping everything in order, there was only one material being. Materialism, therefore, is entirely atheistic.

Modern materialists believe, just like their premodern predecessors, that science always supports materialistic philosophy.

This means science will always accept that all reality and all existence are material. Materialists aren't certain how to explain the human mind. The mind is powerful and therefore remains one of humanity's greatest mysteries. Materialists argue that scientific laws cannot explain the human mind and consciousness. The identity theorists believed the mind could be explained entirely by scientific laws. The opposing views were called property dualists (functionalists), or supervenience andsupervisory theorists.

Modern science is making great strides in unlocking the secrets of the brain. It is now clear that the brain functions much in the same way a computer does. However, the brain performs at much higher levels in many ways. Our brains process information differently to computers. They are multi-dimensional and do not work in a linear fashion. Our consciousness is a multi-dimensional firing process of dumb neurons, brain cells. Is it possible for something that isn't conscious to suddenly become conscious? These are mysteries science still doesn't understand and materialists still struggle to comprehend these concepts. There are many theories and hypotheses that attempt to explain how consciousness arises from matter. Some materialists suggest that non-material entities can cause consciousness in humans, yet they still adhere to science's laws.

Materialists and theists are not alike able to believe in a consciousness that exists after the physical body ceases being alive. This is why they tend to believe in the philosophical view of eternal bliss. This view asserts that there is no consciousness after the death of a materialist. This view has been held both by Roman and Greek philosophers through the years. Socrates is well-known for holding two views. One where the soul/consciousness migrates to another space, living among souls; and the complete cessation or loss of consciousness where the man does not know what is going on and will not. He will never feel pain or suffering again. Socrates is said not to have been able to find peace in either of these theories.

Living in Western society means that we are exposed the teachings from a living spirit, which we can either learn or not. Being materialistic gives you peace of heart knowing it doesn't really matter who God you worshipped or how your life was lived. Your thought chain will be forever broken down and you will no more suffer.

Chapter 5: Why You Should Read This Book, And What It Will Do For You.

Despite being clinically confronted, I have never been too concerned about the moment it is passing. These episodes have helped me understand how I feel about the end of life.

I was well versed in the various stages of Near Death Experiences. This has been supported by serious papers as well as the anecdotic data provided by random publications and inconsistent documentaries. The same holds true for the theories on incarnation as well as reincarnation. This includes the Buddhist concepts that Samsara is only possible if it is not desired.

It was surprising for me to watch close friends react to my experiences as I faced the death process - despite the fact that they had similar levels of understanding. I will share what happens to our consciousness once we die. From the moment the physical body ceases to be ours to the moment when we reincarnate, these are the details from my own personal experience.

I will guide you through the various stages depending on your nature and then share what allows you to move through them. I will describe the experience of these different realms.

To my knowledge, this book has never been published in this manner. This book will have something to offer you.

Dying is the experience of being out of your body

There are many possible ways to die. Natural causes and traumatic deaths may both be possible. Each of these paths can lead to a different outcome, but one thing remains constant: we often dye what we have lived.

Pathology can cause death. The time period between the passing and the next day reflects the change in perceptions of the world. We have a greater appreciation for our surroundings and are more fond of those we know. Light is brighter and the surroundings are as beautiful as ever. At this point, it feels right to say goodbye to everyone, the world and our loved ones. This is the appropriate time for a final affective engagement. Attempting to do it later - which some family members may feel tempted to do- will cause confusion and unnecessary suffering.

A slightly different path will be taken if death occurs as a result from trauma or an incident. Most times, we freeze when we are aware of our imminent doom. Fear is so intense that no pain can be felt. If the body becomes completely unmovable due to fear, terror will flow away into a river filled with goodness and bliss that takes away the flesh.

In both instances, the experience will shift into one that is weightless. Space becomes increasingly tridimensional and all senses are rapidly sorted out to spatial orientation. The perceptions of the self include a representation or our bodily appearance. But, as the sentiment of upwards mobility and pulling increases, so does the perception.

Separation from the physical body causes a gradual loss of consciousness and awareness. Short term memory, awareness and comprehension of who you are and where you were at the time of your passing can become more blurred. However, we may feel indifferent to the circumstances and unaffected by them in most cases.

Ascending through a tunnel into the void

It is possible to ascend through what seems like a tunnel passage, but every person will experience it differently. Cultural references and sensibilities are key factors in determining the nuances. The basic experience will involve travelling through darkness. This is a dark feeling that feels three-dimensional and has a texture that expands to reach every direction. At the end, the tunnel ends.

For those who have experienced a more solid and sensitive awareness, they will be able to point out that they experience clearly distinct stages in their emotions.

The only reason we can travel between different states of existence is to traverse through them. This is best described by the Kabbalistic representation of Tree of Life. We can experience our most precious memories or wishes by being encapsulated in one of the sephirots.

It is here that our nature is reflected in the Universe. The lower spheres can make us experience our own density in an intense way, while Netzach and other spheres will let us sink into the depths of all the love we have, regardless if this nature has been manifested in or during life. This means that the travel experience is not only a purgatory, but also a chance to fulfill our pending wishes and to relive blissful memories of our waking lives.

The amount of our emotional energy to fuel this trip will determine the length of this journey. After the previous stage ends, we can only move on to the next. Transition to the next spehirot will be marked by a change in ambiance and colors, emotions, impressions, and experiences. Unfortunately, our short-term memory can quickly become stale, as we often lose track what we've previously experienced.

This is not possible by willpower, thoughts or willpower. Instead, travel through these spheres relies on our deep nature. Each facet of this state can be expressed. Once we are able to deeply understand ourselves through our experience in Creation, it is now that we can meet other inhabitants.

Chapter 6: The Lords Of Karma

In ancient times people believed that karma was a negative association with evil. This belief was passed from generation to generation, and eventually experts and studies proved that karma has positive side effects.

Finally, the evidence backs what these people claimed. Good deeds are rewarded by good things. There are also claims there are multiple lords to karma. Each with their own set responsibility. Here are some of the most popular karma Lords you should know.

Lords

Paul is considered the master of harmony, even when there is conflict. A testament to his dedication to kindness and goodness is that he was close with Gabriel the Archangel. This makes it obvious that he is one among the karma Lords who can be associated to good.

Kathumi

Kathumi (the second most well-known lord in karma) is now known as the master to the ray of truth, wisdom, love and Divine love. The second is a ray that enshrines the three characteristics required to be successful in life. Kathumi's influence has been a positive one in the lives students, teachers, engineers, and students. Kathumi was also reported to have lived multiple times the life that a human being. Perhaps that is what motivates his concern about the well-being those who maintain society running.

The Lady Portia

Lady Portia does not look like a normal lady. She is charged with balancing judgement and mercy. Simply by looking at Portia you can see how important she is in peoples' lives. She is responsible to help those who have a tendency to judge or criticize others. With all this, we can safely say she is loved by every living being.

Serapis Bay

Serapis Bay may be another lord or lord of good karma. He is known for his compassion and intelligence. He is also known for being the master of the yellow radiation - the third Ray - as he helps philosophers, artists, and all others who are interested in how the world should work together.

Lord Gautama

Lord Gautama, also called the Buddha, has a reputation for providing unwavering wisdom to his followers. Christ is known to be the energy or love because of his responsibilities toward humanity. Lord Gautama, however, is the energy or wisdom.

These are some of the most well-known lords for karma. These are the most powerful lords for karma, judging by what they do.

Self-Mastery and the Degree Of Reincarnation Are Related

E

In other words, volving is the process of advancing from lower to higher levels in life. This belief is supported by the notion that higher divinities are reincarnated from older ones and that perfection can only be achieved through embracing lower levels. Souls evolve from higher levels into souls. They embark on an eternity-long incarnation journey before returning to this world.

When a soul reincarnates it begins to free itself from the confines that are the mental, spiritual, and astral worlds. The soul integrates its characteristics and energy into physical and mental vehicles. The soul spiritualizes and then intentionally burdens the vehicle in order for it to release old karma.

The soul's advancement makes the experience more intense. As they continue to take on a heavier weight with each incarnation, the fourth-degree initiated is subject to the most heavy burden.

This is what explains why the West labels the fourth Reincarnation the "Crucifixion", while the East refers it to the "Great Renunciation". The experience involves the abandonment of every low aspect in order gain a higher spiritual experience.

The Burden Of Karmic Attunement

Folks believe that higher levels of evolution will make karma less restrictive. However this is false. A reincarnated person who has carried the burden of the whole world's history of karma can be more disciplined, world-server and initiate. According to law of Karma sincere disciples serve the world through their service. The more evolved someone is, the more he or she can contribute to the greater good of the whole world.

As a third-degree initiate, the laws and consequences of Karma no long apply to him as he is in control of his destiny. The person transforms into a spiritual consciousness that unconditionally serves the universe, mastering the law and effects of cause and affect and remaining in charge despite having a great Master. This is not an accidental process. Individuals actively participate and are monitored by their incarnated self.

This person is in charge of not only their actions but also their choices. Karma increases their inner view by allowing them access to the physical world.

It is hoped after the fifth initiation that all Karma would be destroyed, resolved, returned to its ultimate source and transformed the individual into an authentic Master.

The Most Powerful and Effective Way To Fix Karma

Individuals are not able to achieve what they desire because that is their way of life. There are many theories about how people's life affects their activities. One of the most common views about this subject is positivism. This theory states that people's actions are unaffected by fate, and is therefore free from any negative consequences. You also have karma.

Karma refers to the direct effect of one's deeds. This broad definition does not support the belief that karma has an intrinsic evil quality. Karma has both good sides and bad. This is inaccurate.

The first is the direct result a good deed. While the second is the result a bad deed. You know that emotions and thoughts are the driving forces behind someone's actions.

They have a direct impact on karma. The following tips will help you avoid bad karma.

Optimism

It is a known fact that over half of humanity is pessimistic. Positive thinking will reduce the chance that you'll experience negative karma. Don't let yourself give up on difficult work as this will make you vulnerable to negative energy. This can have negative results for you and others around the world.

Failure is your only chance to succeed

Many fail to realize the lessons that can come from failure. Although it may seem absurd to some, failure is an important step in the right direction. It is important to not let your failures discourage you. Instead, consider them a learning opportunity that will help you improve. A wise man once said, "A person's life can be likened to an arrow" - meaning that once you have overcome all obstacles imaginable, you'll be ready and able to take your life to greater heights faster than anyone else.

In reality, Patience can be a virtue

Even though patience isn't as valued now as it used to be, it is still vital to practice patience for the knowledge it offers. It doesn't necessarily mean that patience should be associated in any way with sacrifice or forgiveness. It just means everything has a moment. If you don't practice patience or fail to develop patience, you'll have a tendency to go on a rampage whenever you run into a problem. This will most likely lead to horrible karma. You don't want that.

Chapter 7: Memory PreConscience

PreConscience is a stage that begins with several assumptions. First, PreConscience's brain cannot be lost. This is conjecture. It's also reasoned conjecture. PreConscience needs to finish the processes needed to transmit individuality. PreConscience must release the memory-encoded photos before the brain dies. Also, the brain has very limited memory storage.

As was discussed previously, the brain can have as many neuro-synaptic connections or more than there are stars in our universe. To determine which memories are to be transmitted, the limbic must have a method to assess them.

The second is the possibility that PreConscience's transmission ability will be different for each person. PreConscience might not function as intended due to age, trauma or other impairments. Also, the same variables could limit the energy output of the biophoton bursting that releases the memories from our brains at death. It would also affect the consistency of the biophotons.

An example of this is a sinking ship carrying passengers.

Who do we save?

Who do we leave behind?

Although the death of a body is not an imminent sinking ship, it is still a problem: What memories will the body preserve as

PreConscience's and which memories will it forget? How does one make these choices?

PreConscience works with the brain's limbic systems to determine which memories are necessary for preservation of an individual's identity at death. Most of this task would be performed by the amygdala and its emotion control center, the hippocampus. They are both located at the heart of the brain. These components would be the last to go through oxygen loss from cardiac arrest or any physical trauma.

Which memories choose PreConscience to cherish?

This question makes it possible to look at how we are constructed. Let us consider some examples.

Every time we think about our reflection, we feel a shift in our emotions. We either like what the reflection represents or we dislike it. This emotional response is registered by our amygdala. This is called ultra-shortterm memory or sensory. It will fade as the brain's other memories, such as those stored in the cortex, have less impact on it.

Illustration No. Illustration 6. Sensory or ultrashort-term recall can include everything you see, from the clothes and jewelry you wear to how warm and cold you feel and the scents that are being carried by the air.

Illustration No. 6

Working memories don't last long because they have no emotional weight for the neurons to grasp onto. They are the daily flotsam of everyday life. They are caused by the superficial contact that we have with the environment. If the commute to work and home is routine, there's no emotional hook on which it can attach itself to a nerve. The drive to work is the time when we become angry at another motorist's carelessness.

Sometimes, the daily routine can be combined. Each day is different. Every day is different, yet we can take for granted the majority of what happens or what we observe. This is a good example of working memory.

Illustration No. 7

Illustration No. Illustration 7. The difference in sensory memory and working memories is determined by which activity or environment is most important.

For example, in the photo above, the man is seated at a desk and is currently looking at what is on his computer screen. If his wallet is not in the right place, he'll be uncomfortable. This is sensory memories. He has a working memory.

Even after he's forgotten his sore stomach, he'll remember whether he had been rewarded for that report or degraded. His brain's limbic will record his emotional response and the neural connections onto which that memory is encoded.

PreConscience will immediately reject both ultra-short term and working memories. PreConscience has the sole purpose of preserving memories that support individuality. It is therefore impossible to retain much synaptic mass if present sense impressions or day-today working memory. Additionally, the strength and number of the neural-synaptic cellular cells in the amygdala and the hippocampus are key factors in determining which memories are prioritized. They vary in strength and sizes depending on their frequency.

Long-term memories, which are stored in neural-synaptic brain cells, would be more robust and longer-lasting than any recently created memories. This could be because they have been around for longer periods of time and were used more often. To evaluate this, the limbic would need to perform a simple computation.

All it would take for the limbic systems to compare the strength or size of synapses in each long term memory is that they receive. CSF washing would allow long-term memories and ions to escape into the neural system upon cardiac arrest. These ions-held memories are then sent to the amygdala where they can be used to prioritize emotional behavior according to size-comparison.

The limbic system is faced with a much more challenging task: distinguishing between long-term, equal-sized or near-equal-sized memories. How does PreConscience pick which long-term experiences to save?

These memories, which we often don't even try to recall, are our strongest long-term memory. They are like phantoms rising from the subconscious. Images of distant events are flooding our minds like a motion movie we can't stop watching or ignoring. They seem able to dominate our attention, regardless of what we're doing right now.

Evolution created PreConscience in order to conserve information that would conform with fundamental physical laws. As individuals, we do not know what each other is. We are not the observer who watches us fall, but the object behind our face as we slide down the canyon ledge into mist.

Our conscious mind is held captive by our second-to, or even third-sensual experience and the requirements of our daily lives. Long-term memory generation is a program that runs deep in our subconscious.

PreConscience's mystical component is found at the time of long-term memory generation and prioritization. These two seemingly contradictory concepts are combined. It is important to feel good when creating memories that last longer and are stronger.

Recent research supports this theory. It was found that the brain's Amygdala controls how the brain preserves emotional memories. This happens by encoded upon our memories the emotions that we experience as we live our lives. Emotions can have both long-term and transient effects on your memory. Emotionally charged memories such as those involving words, faces and pictures are more likely to be recalled than memories that are emotion-neutral.

This research confirms that emotions are loaded into our memories by the amygdala. Furthermore, it supports a vital physiological step in PreConscience's operation.

In 2003, another team of researchers looked at the effects negative emotions had on long-term memory. The results showed that long-term memories are stronger and more durable than any other memories. In addition, long-term memories are more likely to be remembered than short-term.

One hypothesis is that long-term negative memories are more powerful than long-term positive memories. Therefore, synapses which contain long-term negative long-term experiences have stronger ions and are physically larger. This tendency to remember negative emotions over other long-term memories may be an evolutionary design for survival. It is possible evolution has boosted the ionic presence of negative or potentially life-threatening memories in synapse to help preserve itself.

PreConscience cannot function properly if there is a gradual loss in brain oxygen. All the necessary processes to download prioritize, encode and transmit memories need to be completed before PreConscience runs out oxygen. This time limit makes it easier than it seems.

Because the amygdala can encode emotion upon memories, it makes sense that it should also possess an emotional matrix. It could serve as a blueprint for the person's personal identity, and even a map of how they have changed over the years. This makes perfect logical sense because PreConscience has to exist in order for it to transmit emotions to memory and encode both upon biophotons.

If this is the case, the amygdala will only need to run long-term memories over its own emotional matrix in order to prioritize ions. It would then keep memories that match it and discard those that don't. These remaining prioritized ion-held memories carrying the person's individuality-encoded memories would then be transferred to another area of the limbic system for biophoton encoding.

MEMORY ENCODING

Three components are required to encode memory

1. The ions containing memories

2. A location in the limbic where the memories are successfully encoded.

3. This is the transmission medium upon which the memories will be emitted from your body.

Already, it has been described how the ion held memories are likely to be prepared. Encoding ion-held memory must be performed electrochemically. It can employ the same principles used in simple photography, but it could also use more advanced techniques such as magnetic resonance imaging. Whatever the process used, it must be consistent with the brain's natural physiology and require minimal time and energy. These two parts would be lost if a person dies. Gray matter and white matter in the brain may have already been "dead", and perhaps the brain's center, where lies the limbic, is the only part that is still viable.

The limbic system is responsible for encoding memories to transport out of body. It must be free from any electrical activity that could cause interference with PreConscience. To ensure stable encoding, this area must be organized. It would also need to be relatively free of cellular activity of its own--a relatively electrochemically-free zone within which the encoding could take place in the same way a darkroom is necessary to develop photographic film. Because cellular activity within the brain at this stage in the death process will be significantly reduced, or absent, some interference may be acceptable.

One area of the brain that fulfills all of these requirements is called the hippocampal

Sulcus. This pocket, or fissure, lies within the hippocampal formation just near the Amygdala. The hippocampal (or hippocampal) sulcus contains the two essential qualities required to encode PreConscience memories.

Its pocket-like form allows it to easily hold and stabilize ionized memories while they are being encoded onto a transport medium. The hippocampal sulfur is also relatively free of cells. This allows for PreConscience to encode in an area without interference from electrochemical activity.

Illustration No. 8

How do memories get encoded?

Illustration No. Illustration 8. The hippocampal, or pocket-like, fold is shown in the drawing. It lies between the subiculum and the dentate.

The brain's "little darkroom" is the hippocampal. The pocket at the fold creates the compactness needed to hold together the biophotons with the ionized memories. There is a brief flash of lighting as the biophotons, memory-ions and biophotons combine. The memories are bioelectrically transferred like photographs from the photons to the ions. Once the memories have been "flash-encoded", the biophotons become free and can travel outside the body.

Ion-held memories in the amygdala that prioritize ions would not travel far to reach their hippocampal sulfurcus, as the hippocampus is right below it. The pocket-like formation in the sulcus would hold the ions in place long enough to allow the hippocampus release a flashes of biophotons.

This may be what causes the sudden and intense EEG burst seen by ER doctor treating patients who suffered near-death experiences. This flashing of biophotons will extend through the surrounding hippocampal Sulcus tissue, creating a Holographic Image of the memories stored in the ions. The 360-degree flashes from biophotons could also be used to encircle ion-held memories and provide the energy and data coherence needed for survival in the event of an ion-related emission.

Recent years have witnessed biophoton emission from humans becoming a popular area of research. The evidence is growing that photons play an integral role in the fundamental functioning of cells. The light from photons is emitted by cells when they are active and used to communicate with other cells. Photons may also play a crucial role in neural functioning. In rats, light has been observed from the spinal neurons. Microtubules within the brain could be thought to function as optical fibers, carrying photonic data.

Apart from electrical and chemical signals that propagate in neurons of the brains, signal propagation also occurs in the form biological photons. Researchers have confirmed the photon-guiding property of a single nerve cell by performing experiments. Interactions among microtubules, biophotons, and the brain could cause fluctuations and transitions of the tubules from coherent to noncoherent states.

Biophysics' exciting new field of biophysics merits attention.77

As Professor Majid Rahnama (Iran's Shahid Bahonar University) suggests:

Rhanama & his research group suggest:

"These interactions involve long distance ionic wave propagation through microtubule networks, AFs (action filaments), and subcellular control ionic channel activation 78

They argue that microtubules can be considered to be biological electrical dipoles. They believe that microtubules can also be considered to be biological electrical dpoles.

Other researchers also confirmed the existence and presence of biophotons within human brains. Professor Joey M. Caswell's team taught human subjects how to use intent to alter the direction of "random number generators" within a special device that was located within 1 meter from the test subjects. This device captured biophoton emissions of the brain's right side and recorded each subject's thoughts simultaneously.

Caswell discovered that photon emission rose significantly when subjects tried to alter the numbers generated randomly by the random generator. These photon-emitting thoughts were likely caused by intentional thought patterns, according the researchers. These photons were therefore attributed to the human brain as part of its normal processes.

Independent scientific teams have documented the relationship between the biophoton emissions and the hippocampus. Nicolas Rouleau, Biomolecular Scientist Program at Laurentian University Sudbury, Ontario Canada, measured biophotons that exceeded background field densities (electromagnetic force densities), in hippocampal tissue cuts of and in the brains human test subjects engaged with specific thought processes.

Rouleau performed a separate study that found that human brain tissue from the hippocampal region had the ability of emitting biophotons 20-years after death.

A 2016 study also found that glutamate induced biophotonic activities, transmissions and activities in the brain, present an spectral redshift from animals (in alphabetical order: bullfrogs mice, chickens pigs and monkeys) towards humans. This shift is even higher than the near-infrared wavelength in human brain. They believe that the increased photonic activity in the human mind may partly explain the high intelligence and efficiency of humans.

For decades, scientists have debated the topic of quantum mechanical brain processes. However, biophoton emission is now observed in real time and can be studied. It is proven. It is proven that the brain emits continuous biophotons as part its normal everyday function. The conclusion that human brains are a continuous source biophotons because of their electrochemical or electromagnetic processes is quite startling. This biophotonic behavior also opens the door for the astounding reality that our brains are organic quantum mechanical machines.

Brain physiology creates and uses quantum mechanical energy.

Chapter 8: Facts Of Life And Afterlife

There are certain facts that are vital to the concept of Reincarnation. These facts are believed by most people who have a religious belief. They are still seen with suspicion in the West. This is due to an increase in logical positivism across western circles. Western sceptics believe that science is the only path to genuine knowledge. The exploration of other forms of knowledge is not recommended. Science is one of the most important channels of knowledge. But it isn't the only channel. Although scientifically incontestable, the channel of Reincarnation can provide us with a spiritual knowledge that can transform our lives.

Reincarnation begins with the belief that there is a soul. It's more than a myth. All human beings possess a soul. Humans have two natures. One part of that dual nature includes the physical aspect, our mortal coil. The other part of that nature is the immortal and indestructible soul.

This soul is what gives life its essence. It is the only valid solution to the existential problem of "Who are I?".

This soul is not static. It's constantly evolving and learning. It's part the spirit so it naturally becomes self-aware. The soul evolves by expressing itself and becoming more aware of its surroundings. The soul is able to evolve, and so does consciousness. The purpose for reincarnation is, therefore, to improve the human consciousness.

The physical medium that we experience is the most effective medium for the evolution and maintenance of our souls is the material reality. Our personal, subjective experiences influence the shape of our souls. The soul expands when it makes independent decisions. This is because it learns to better know itself. You can learn more about yourself by making those choices.

The soul has to incarnate within a human body in order to experience this experience. It is fused with a bodily existence, most often a human one, from birth to the end. The soul evolves through the experiences in these human bodies. The soul experiences separation when it is in the human form. This is something that it has never experienced before it was united to the Spirit. It experiences the Otherness that is entailed in human existence. This is essential for the growth of the soul.

It's vital for the soul that it experiences all human emotions. One soul might be a victim of another reincarnation while another may be a us. It may reincarnate in a male and female body at the same time. Therefore, the soul doesn't have any nationality. It's all one. Many believe that, after three consecutive births of the exact same gender, one can get a reincarnation. However, this is not a strict rule.

The way the soul learns is by comparing and contrast. The soul's greatest learning tool is to compare different situations. This is fundamentally the purpose behind reincarnation. The lessons we are going to learn in this life time depend on where we were born and what our race is. Sometimes, the soul will choose that. Sometimes, it's an accident.

Not doing good deeds, or having good karma will necessarily eliminate bad karma. Learning requires suffering, which is something the soul actively opts to do before it begins its human life. It is necessary for a soul to experience pain in this life. Buddha affirms that life can be difficult and can cause suffering. It can't be other way.

There are some teachings that claim we only receive the human reincarnation if we go through 8,400,000 other physical incarnations. The distance our soul travels to reach the human life is immense. Only the souls human beings are capable of salvation.

The soul is conscious about what experiences and choices it will make in the next life before the reincarnation occurs. Spirit is active to guide the soul. Before the reincarnation starts, the circumstances and timings of these events are determined. It will therefore experience the opposite of compassion, in order to acquire the ability to love children. It may experience neglect, abandonment, or violence at the hands of its nearest guardians. This soul then has to accomplish the opposite: to find compassion and overcome grief.

The conditions are thus pre-planned. Our fate is determined by how we respond to these conditions.

Reincarnation cannot be described as a wheel that continues on. It's not one-way traffic. It is a common belief. This circle is permanent and unending. It is a circle that will keep you bound and there is no escape from it. Endless death, rebirth, and reincarnation are not, strictly speaking.

Once you reach a certain level, your journey to reincarnation will have a beginning and an ending. When we reach that level, the bonds of human form are broken free. We become part and parcel of the Spirit, the goal of reincarnation. To evolve from love is the spirit behind every lifetime.

Contrary the popular belief, there is no pressing need to be enlightened and complete our reincarnation. There is no urgent need to learn. Time is not a concept that exists in the cosmic view. We must all learn at our own pace. The physical world is not always a pitiful place. It's important not to grow out of a hurry, but out of love.

After death, we do not immediately reincarnate to another physical life. Traditions tell us that we have interactions with other souls, and can learn from them. A soul must complete seven stages before it can be eligible for reincarnation in the human body. When all conditions are in place, we can be born again.

Chapter 9: Further Study Of Old Souls And New Souls

The Arizal explained more about the concept that new souls are different from old souls. Very few souls were not included in Adam's soul. These souls are called entirely new souls. All souls which are included in Adam's soul are known as old souls.

There are three levels in relation to Adam's soul: a. New souls are souls that are not part of Adam's soul. The organs of Adam's body became smaller after he sinned. They were now only 100 amoth (about 125 feet). Cain & Abel were created from the sparks left over after the sin. c. Adam's soul lost the sparks it had after the sin. They fell into the hands and feet of Klipoth, evil forces. Seth, Adam's child, was created from these sparks.

This level of soul is called completely new. It descends into this realm and into a human body. The Nefesh born can reach the lowest level known as Neshama or Atziluth, achieving level after level in a single life. This new soul will have to return to the earth as an old spirit if it sins and is blemished. At the time that the soul is born, the Ruach comes at the age thirteen years, and eventually the Neshama at twenty years. The soul's actions determine its development until it can reach Naran at Zilut.

The second layer is the sparks that remained after Adam's sin and were passed to Cain/Abel when they were babies. These souls are also brand new souls. However, they are not entirely new. These souls passed on to Abel, Cain, and their offspring are not considered reincarnated. This is unlike other souls which die in one body, but are reincarnated elsewhere. These souls can be considered part of Adam's legacy that he has allowed his sons to inherit. Thus, souls from Cain and Abel that were part of the souls of Adam are considered to have been withered from the soul. These souls come from Adam, Cain or Abel and are united with the body of Adam. However, they are not new. Cain and Abel were able to inherit these sparks. It was considered a partial come. This soul dies when it sins, leaving a mark, and becomes reincarnated.

This partly new soul, when it comes into the world, is able to attain Nefesh from Asiyah Ruachof Yetzirah Neshamaof Beriah Nefeshof Atziluth. It is not capable of reaching the Neshama Atziluth-level like a completely fresh soul. The reason why there is a difference between the totally new soul (part of Adam) and the fully new soul (part of the soul of Adam), is that Adam lost the supernal radiation, also called Naranchy. The Naranchy, Atziluth, departed above their place and did not fall into the hands of the external forces that are evil. These forces of evil only have an influence in the three lower universes Beriah Yetzirah or Asiyah. They do not have any influence in Atziluth. Only the Nefesh Atziluth was left after Adam's sin. This is the light that supernal radiatance shines. Therefore, the sparks found in Cain and Abel fall into the bodies of man. They can only achieve the Nefesh status of Atziluth by their deeds. The totally new souls, known as the supernal Radiance, have the potential to attain the Naranchy at Ziluth.

Another difference between the potentiality of the completely newly created soul and that of the old soul is the fact that the new, completely complete soul can achieve all the heights and radiances without excessive effort or difficulty. The new, incomplete soul reaches Nefesh Atziluth through great effort and toil as well as by reciting the night sentence "My soul will seek you out at the night."

Sometimes, if an individual completes the corrections of his Nefesh with the sentence "I would search you out in the night," he can draw down a Ruach during the day so that his Ruach corrects the second body. After that, he will be able reunite with the first Nefesh. The same applies to Neshama.

Many righteous people die young, because they have already corrected their souls in a few decades and don't know how you bring a Ruach through Neshama's recital of "my spirit will seek you out". This is what happens to partially complete new people. Because the souls are completely unblemished and new, the Ruach/Neshama can simply enter the Nefesh of the completely new ones.

Also, completely new souls cannot attain the Neshama Atziluth level. This is a difference from completely new ones. Nefesh when you are born until thirteen years and one-day later. Then Ruach until age 20. To reach Neshama, Atziluth at age

20, it will take 120 years. The advantage of the not completely new spirit is that it can attain Nefesh or Atziluth status before the age 13. It can also achieve this status one day, according its intentions and actions.

The third level is made up of those souls that were enslaved by the forces of evil outside of Adam's sin. Seth, Adam's son was born out these sparks. These souls have been called old souls. They are, in all respects, lower than other souls. These sparks had lost their soul and were now separated into many sparks. They are therefore referred to as reincarnated souls if they appear for the first time in the body. This reincarnation, which is considered a second, will occur when the soul dies. These souls are called old souls and cannot complete all levels.

The only difference between the second level new souls attached the souls Adam Cain and Abel is that the Ruach in the new souls Cain/Abel can't leave the depths or

Klipoth of the evil force, or Klipoth until their Nefesh becomes complete. It is not possible for him, or any other soul, to correct his Ruach. So either the man dies and the Ruach will be repaired in another body, or he will draw down Ruach by reciting, "My soul shall seek you out during the night", and drawing down Ruach at the time that he falls asleep in exchange for his Nefesh. The third level of the souls is Seth. These souls have the ability to draw the Ruach down even before they have fully repaired the Nefesh. It is done when the souls from Seth pray at the time Nefilat Apaim and then they prostrate in supplication. The Ruach may descend into another man's bodies through the Nefesh for a stranger. If he is able to merit, he will be able to bring down through Nefilat Apaim, "falling in prayer" a Ruach born to him. To be able to receive the Neshama, you cannot bring it down through "falling onto the face" in prayer. The person must have completed his Nefesh/Ruach before he can die.

A Ruach can be drawn into the world as a Nefesh to assist an old soul to God by falling on his face in prayer and following recital of Amidah. This Ruach from Eden can be given to this man's body. It will then have the full Nefesh of the Ruach who caused a new Ruach into the world. This can only be done if the Ruach that this man had received from the Garden was complete before the Nefesh to the man who had prayed and made supplication.

The Nefesh was the one who caused the Ruach to unite with the Nefesh for the stranger, and is now able to merit the Ruach's good deeds. However, at Resurrection, all of the Nefesh's and Ruach's portions will be given to the stranger who changed his ways. This will happen if either soul is more meritorious than the other. If they are equally meritorious, then one of them will sin. If the first soul sins, the second soul with its merits can correct that sin and return it by repentance and doing good deeds. The Ruach of one soul can be redeemed by the Ruach and the Nefesh the other souls, because they have been drawn together from Seth's soul. Ahab and Yerboam, who were souls, are a good example. Even though they did not do the same deeds as each other, their souls were almost equal. They were half good and half wicked. They fell to idolatry sometimes, but their souls remained half right and half wrong. God always directed them to repent. Elijah was the prophet who chased them after righteousness until finally they were enslaved by Nevoth, the Israeli.

The Arizal taught King David that his soul was very high. The sin of Adam made the soul of David sink into the darkest depths of the outside forces of evil. This was the first occasion that these sparks had been seen from the Klipoth. David's soul started from Nefesh in Asiyah as he was a third-level soul reincarnation. This is to say that David's soul was formed from a very strong spark that had fallen to the outside forces of evil. Now, the Nefesh has escaped the evil forces. It descended into King David's physical body at the time it was born as a reincarnated old spirit. The prayer "Nefilat Apaim" allowed the Ruach to be drawn into another body. King David, however, sinful with the daughter from Sheba, had his soul and body blemished, which would have received both the Nefesh (and Ruach) at the time the Resurrection. David lost his salvation as a result of this sin. Psalms makes it clear that David was not saved by God Selah because he sinned along with Sheba's child.

Chapter 10: The Nature Of Past Lives

There are many opinions about the nature of past-life phenomena. Mixed with a rich past of religions, superstitions, personal preferences, scientific discourse, and flights-of-fantasy, the opinions regarding our past life and afterlife are as varied and diverse as the people who own them.

Types of past lives ideologies

The majority of people believe that past lives are merely tangible lives that our souls experienced. This idea is common and suggests that our soul is infinitely able to return again and again into this human world in different forms. Some believe there is an evolutionary process that takes us from primitive to more advanced complex existences over time. Some others enjoy the idea and practice of karma. They believe that our reincarnated form can be determined by the karmic goals we have achieved in our different life journeys.

There are many other ideas about the nature of our souls reincarnated. Some believe all our existences are tied together in a form of cosmic consciousness. Sometimes called an akashic Record. This consciousness includes intimate details of all our incarnations (past, present, and upcoming) as well the essence of all reality. Many people who support the idea of the Akashic Records try to get in touch with his higher consciousness in an effort to expand their minds.

Some believe that all of us live simultaneously in a multidimensional present. Accessing past life memories is as easy as reaching across a cosmic divide and extracting information regarding another aspect. This idea is very similar in concept to the solipsist mentality, which is difficult to accept for many. Solipsist philosophy holds that only mind is possible --- your mind.

Your mind is the core of all reality, and everything else is a reflection or fragment of yours. While the solipsist perspective is not easy for many, it's something I suspect to be close to the truth. It's only my opinion. I tend towards the belief that all things and thoughts and consciousness are one. Each object is merely a reflection, or an outreach of one consciousness. It doesn't really matter if the world is made up of me or the consciousness I created it. It is not important to make the distinction. The distinction is irrelevant.

Past lives, religion

Nearly every major religion has some connection with the idea of past life. Many major religions have become less recognizable as core beliefs. If you do a thorough search of the religious sources, you will find strong allusions in many religions to reincarnation theories. Google can be used to find numerous examples in

Christian literature with hints about reincarnation.

To learn more about your own life history

Why are you interested in learning more about past lives, especially your own?

It started out as pure curiosity, at least for me. I was a 20year-old college student who wanted to know more. So I was invited to a past lifetime regression session. My entire knowledge of past lives could have been summarized by watching a few 80s movies or television programs. I will admit, I was excited about the chance to go through my past lives again. It was great. In fact, I was very impressed.

My Past Experiences, My Life

I recall being invited to come back on the couch with my therapist. She dimmed her lights and started playing soft, soothing music. She let out a whiffling of incense, and began leading me through my regression. As we started, I was skeptical. In the next 10-15 minutes, I noticed a shift in my attitude. It was unbelievable. I kept finding I was becoming lost in her voice, the ambience around me, my own thoughts, and even my own thoughts. Although I was drifting off a bit, I was still fully present.

Many unfamiliar images appeared as I was led towards the regression session. My life before that point was filled with everyday things, which is typical for a 20year-old. I was very interested and passionate about college courses. I was obsessed by music. I was passionate about my friendships and my relationships. I would have hoped that a past lifetime fantasy would have carried me to something more exciting, perhaps related to my current area of study (the science). But what I remembered was so much more.

I was slowly guided to my past life. I can recall it clearly, even though it was over a decade ago. I was a journalist and newspaperman of low rank in a small

European community. It was the dawn of the twenty-first century. Although there were many global concerns such as war and disease, my life was quite ordinary and far from the global dramas. I vividly remembered many highlights in my life, including possibly the first time that I got behind the wheel. Although it couldn't reach 20 mph at all, I felt as though I was racing in 100. Driving was a new experience for me. The wind in my hair, the freedom to go anywhere I want to and the excitement that new technologies offer, all of this was incredible to me. This was clearly a shadowed experience by the birth of my children. I was happy, productive, and married. There were many tragedies in my life. There were also more concerns about the future. It was a full life of details, trials, and tribulations. It was a whole life. It was a life. It felt real and human. Many of these details remain vividly in my mind to this day.

So why do you bother with the trouble?

There are other reasons you might look into your own past lives. Regression clients are often interested in exploring their past lives for many reasons. I've seen this many times over the years. My second favorite reason people are interested in understanding why they are here is not the above-mentioned curiosity. They want to see if their lives in the past have had any influence on the present. Many of these people suffer with anxiety or depression. They believe that understanding their history will help them to deal with the present. The trend in depression and anxiety is that people with anxiety and panic disorder report experiencing traumatic events in the past.

As I write this, my mind is brought back to a friend who lost his family in a horrible fire. He was in an enormous house in central Europe, during the winter. An accident happened and the house was set on fire. He might have managed to escape but his family remained inside. He was trying to reach his kids. He failed his attempts, and it is likely that the entire family lost their lives that night. He is still anxious about being separated from his loved ones and worries that his overprotection of his children causes him anxiety.

These memories revealed that the gentleman claimed that his anxiety had decreased over the next few months. I'm not sure if this was because he became less protective about his children. However, I believe that he did find some comfort in knowing the probable and likely source of his discomfort.

Another client who was also suffering from depression and anxiety throughout his entire life claimed that he has uncovered memories of himself living in a small cabin away from society. He believed he was grotesque, deformed, and unlovable. He was the scariest old man, about whom children would tell scary stories to each other. The man today is quite good-looking, very financially stable, highly talented, and intelligent. But he still seems to struggle from the backlash of his former life. It's likely been 15 years since his regression. He often recounts the story to my friends and tells them about the time. After the experience, he feels more at home in his own skin and is less self-hating.

One of the most surprising trends I've seen in past life regressions is people being shocked by what they find. It's a joke that everyone arrives dressed as Cleopatra to a past-life themed costume party. Everybody makes assumptions about what their past lives were like. Surprisingly many people return with memories from past lives that are very surprising. Instead of being a princess or a prince, many people find themselves living an ordinary life in a small tribe. According to the rule of thumb, a dull existence seems to be the norm. It is true that every life has highlights and drama. However, the vast majority of lives -

whether present or future – are simply ordinary. There have been hundreds of thousands years of human culture in the world, many generations without anything significant. Every life is filled with triumphs and tragedies. These can be easily recalled during the past lives regression session. Most people are not surprised by the existence of a mundane person in a place or time with no historical significance. One example is that they might be interested and knowledgeable about Civil War history, but are surprised to discover that their past lives were as simple French peasants in the 1300s. Cleopatra might not be possible for everyone.

Past life alternatives

It would be dishonest for someone to suggest that there is no alternative to the past lives narrative. It is almost impossible to determine the veracity or authenticity of past-life memories. There are numerous cases that people have linked past life memories to real people or real places through past-life regressions. Newspapers and obituaries have been used by these people to verify their memories. These are rare exceptions. The lack of details and the length of time they were supposed to have occurred means that most of the past life memories are difficult to confirm. Bavaria 1450 A.D. did not have many reliable newspapers to confirm the specific lives of people.

What are some possible alternatives? Some people believe guided meditation opens the door into "imagination space", where people are given the chance to fill out the blanks through directed, but open-ended questions. Let's say that I am leading you through a hypnotic guided Meditation and suggest that I ask you what color car you see. You would have to answer this question because it is consistent with the original statements. Perhaps you see a blue car ....or even a truck. You are simply fulfilling your instructor's expectations.

This phenomenon, known as false memory Syndrome (FMS), is well-known in psychological and psychotherapy communities. FMS can cause people to remember events that never took places. FMS issues have caused many witnesses to be declared completely unreliable in a number of cases. Many stories were told about ritual satanic violence cases in the 1980s or 1990s. It seems that the phenomenon has spread somewhat. Many of these cases were about alleged victims of satanic abuse who recovered their memories through hypnosis. Often, they had poor hypnotists. Investigators were often unsuccessful in verifying claims of abuse or other potential crimes. For example, a victim might claim they were abused by New York City's satanic community while their Montana family had never been away. Investigators would often discover

People can be very good at filling the blanks with their memories in order to please the therapist. This process is documented in numerous scientific journals. This should be considered in light of the possibility past life memories might not be entirely legitimate.

The truth is that each individual must decide whether the memories they uncover are valid. After many years of providing regression sessions I feel that the quality or the truth of the memory is an indicator of its reality. You can't just expect the therapist to remember everything.

Another popular viewpoint is one that I don't agree with. Many believe that it doesn't matter whether the experience was created or real. Many people believe that the psychological value of working through the memories from deep inside the subconscious is worth the effort. While I appreciate the therapeutic effect, my curious side is more concerned with the truthfulness of the memories. It is up to you, the individual, to determine if the memories have any truth or importance.

Chapter 11: Depression, Inner And Spiritual Healing

Anxiety disorders, which affect around 264 million people in the world, have been one of the most common mental health problems. Depression and related mental disorders are the most common cause of incapacity among people aged 15 to 44. Anxiety has increased exponentially since the SARS outbreak, and a higher number of people are at risk. Hypnotherapy can treat mental health disorders. Because it is comfortable for the relaxed mind, hypnosis is soothing and can relieve symptoms such as anxiety and depression. The benefits include emotional stability, stress reduction, positive worldview and more control of one's life.

Hypnosis Session. Inner Healing and Optimism

You will need to find somewhere you are comfortable enough to either sit or lay down ....

Take a deep inhale and slowly exhale.

Keep taking a deep, slow breath. Hold the position for 3 seconds ..... Release slowly.

Inhale the air and oxygen as it slowly fills your body.

Observe how the air enters your body with each inhale .... Slowly exhale.

The tension is a way to abandon your body.

Breathe in again.............and let go......

You're falling into a state that is almost like a stupor, enjoying the calm of your own inner world.

Imagine yourself lying on a sunbed on a warm summer's afternoon.

The hot blue sky and clouds make you feel drowsy..................... drowsier than you have ever felt before....

Imagine the warmth melting away all of your problems and replacing it with positive fuel, vitality and energy from the sunlight.

It's like a ray, of technicoloured, gloriously pure sunlight shining brightly inside you. It's as though the feeling of joy and happiness is growing beautifully, filling your whole being.

Don't let the heat get to you

Completely let the go

You will experience a sense of calm and comfort when I count from ten-to-one.

You are soaking in the light from the glorious golden sun.

Ten, you are charging every cell in your body with exuberance.

Nine, let us go! Let us plunge into the safety net, which will provide security and reassurance.

Eight, you feel completely and completely relaxed right now.

Feel the life-giving intensity of life, pulsing through your veins and infiltrating your thoughts.

Sleepy........peaceful......pleasantly drowsy as you are, you can still simultaneously acknowledge where your spirit is going,

Seven, the generously-cozy, tranquil properties awaken inside your unconscious essence. They touch every fibre of your mind, overflowing and spreading celestial power through your entire body.

Six. Fully relaxed.

You are strong, courageous, and ready to unleash all of the potential you have. The power you have hidden within you is there, waiting for you to unleash it to propel you forward.

Five, warmer .... the warmer .... the deeper you go ...... it's as if your body is in hibernation. It's like being immersed in the stimulating sunshine, overflowing into your core .... making it so satisfying, so nourishing.

Four, you are at absolute tranquility, an aura full of light, protection, and light surrounds you.

These shapes sparkle and shimmer, and the particles falling randomly scatter them.

Three. You close your eyes. Now, hold your hands open wide and let the amazing energy bits gently fall into your palms.

Two, when you look down at you hands, you can see how the elements are changing and morphing together, creating a new shape.

It transforms into soft, silky feathers.

One, it transforms into an elegant white dove. As it gracefully flies from your palm, it gently flaps her wings.

It glides uphill, gently brushing against you with its elegant feathers. It feels so calming, so smooth and fluffy.

As the dove is near your head, you can feel your body shrink. The quills of the birds grow larger and larger.

You can close your eyes to feel the delicate silk texture underneath your body. It wraps itself around your body.

As the fascinatingly charming creature perches through the sky, you are astonished to see it.

It slowly descends through a cloud to come back down ...... under the mist. From there, it cruises steadily at the same level.

The wind blows through your hair. After you have taken a deep relaxing breath in .... you can look down.

What can we see?

What are you able to see from this spectacular bird's eyes view?

You can clearly see all of the forests, lanes, paths, as well as people, cars, streets, and houses.

You are witnessing the wonderful road map of you own life from a transcendental angle.

It's the spiritual side of you stepping outside your body.

From up high you can see everything that you had forgotten, both good and evil.

All the things, which have caused you great pain and made you feel numb, are the things that you have disconnected from.

It is possible to clearly see the things you are feeling uneasy or sad about. You can also see your fears and hopes.

It's like the roots of trees, with each stem leading to a unique path.

Each stem represents you. The tree represents .... your past, present, future. It is one and the same entity within these lives. Time and space are irrelevant.

Although it appears like one tree and one life, beneath the surface this tree contains the memories of all your lives. Deep beneath the soil is your memory, which you can access at any time. .... any memory that you wish can be uncovered and recalled. This will help you heal from the scars and find peace.

It's all interconnected. They are all waiting for your retrieval.

Take a moment ....

That thought is ......

Now, I'll be announcing my countdown from five to one.

As I guide you, absorb all suggestions that I make to that portion of you that is responsible in bringing this to life. You will see past lives clearly and close up. This will allow you to open your subconscious, or sleeping mind, to the previous experience.

Five, let go of any doubts or doubts that may be in your mind. Let yourself drift and float until you return to the first memory you can recall. Use the power and guidance of your senses.

You can see what there is. ....Take some time allow yourself to recall nostalgic moments

Are you in a garden, a park, a woodland, or forest? You are in a yard, park, forest, or woodland?

What's the weather like today?

Is it a sunny, clear spring or Summer day? Or is it rainy and cold?

Who is the one with you? Do you recognize this individual? Do you recognize this person when you are in a building of any kind?

What do you see in yourself? What are you like? What is the style of your hair? What colors are you able see?

Four,

What can we hear?

Can you hear people talking, laughing or crying?

Is music on? Perhaps you can hear a single instrument? Maybe you are the one actually playing it.

You might be able hear the sounds of nature. The trees gently move in the breeze. Birds singing and tweeting. Are there grasshoppers that chirp? Is it the sound of rain or waves washing up on shore?

Three,

What do you feel on your skin?

Can you feel a breeze blowing through your hair, the cool rain droplets on your face, or the warmth of the sun kissing your skin?

Pay attention what surface you are standing upon. Are you wearing footwear?

Is the ground hot or cold below you?

Two,

What can smell?

Imagine your familiar scents, ... fragrances that can connect you to a specific place, object, or individual. Perhaps it's the sweetness of flowers, the perfume or aftershave a person uses, or even the scent of freshly cut grass.

One,

Your sense of taste ...... Pay attention to how your brain is able to recall certain flavours.

Is there a meal that you are most fond of?

Are you walking along a sandy beach while eating icecream? Are you feeling hungry or just walking along a beach? Who are your eating companions? Who may have prepared and cooked a meal?

Take a second to consider ....

Surfacing now in your innermost thought are powerful intense feelings of healing. It is turning back the clock for any thoughts that lead to sadness or depression.

As though you are going back in time to see where it all started, as if your mind is traveling back in time to locate the origin of the anxiety.

Feel the warmth of the sun illuminating the darkness and sending away any shadows that may be casting a shadow.

Your entire body feels radiant and full of life. You're eradicating the negative emotions. It is replaced with a new shining optimism.

Chapter 12: Joining The Ancestors

The transition from this existence to another is the most important aspect of the relationship with the dead , and it must be considered. In this chapter, you'll have to think about your own mortality, and what you'd like to be remembered after you die. The roles that the four elements (fire water, wind as well as earth) in rituals that care for the body following death, as well as in the symbolism surrounding life after death will be addressed. The chapter ends with suggestions for offering assistance during funerals, understanding the different stages of the post-death experience and recognizing the anniversary of one year since the passing of a loved one.

Death Preparation

If we're asked to think about the possibility

of our own demise and the possibility of a peaceful death, we naturally fantasize about being surrounded by beloved family members at the end of our lives, slowly releasing ourselves from our body, suffering only. There are a few of us who appreciate a different version of this fairy tale ending known as the "good end." Personally, I'm not convinced that the completion of the inner work of living as an ethical and conscious human being is in any way connected with the time and method of our deaths. To think otherwise is to believe that, unlike others having influence over your death as well as how fate and destiny operate. But the overwhelming evidence shows that even good and pure people die young, in shocking, unpredictably horrifying ways. For the majority people, the death may be sudden, taking the form of grief or fear, and in states far from being lucid. It's not about receiving what we deserves and dying isn't about punishment or punishment, at least not in the majority of circumstances. The next section is based on an ideal situation with a few relatively pain-free months to prepare yourself for death.

Months to go

If you are worried that you'll end up dying within the next few months, you should take good care of your own relations and affairs prior to taking a skydiving trip or an esoteric journey to distant lands. This includes taking care of your financial and legal holdings, and deciding what will happen to your personal possessions. All of these concerns are easily solved by writing a will; however, only about half of Americans have ever done it. People who have been faced with the financial and legal concerns when grieving may appreciate the importance of writing the final will and testament in advance of the date. Do you have some items you'd like to be buried or cremated while thinking about what will happen to your the personal possessions you have? Are there any items of a ceremonial nature that need to be passed down to other people in your family or require special attention? I have heard stories about the confusion and emotional turmoil regarding the care and treatment of my friend's sacred instruments and spirit bundles after she died suddenly in 2006. With the help of online resources, a will which addresses the issues is usually written within a matter of hours. If you experience untimely death it will provide an enormous amount of peace of mind for your loved ones. It's also at a minimum it helps to keep up with your day-to-day tasks.

You could also perform the last rites you want when you are prepared. Are you clear on what you would like to be done to your body when you're gone? Do you want your eyes closed for you in case you were to die with them open? Would you like to give your organs or entire body for medical research? Would you like to have your body cleaned or dressed in according to a specific way prior to being cremated or buried? Would you like an honoring vigil or other ceremonies performed by your loved relatives in the days following your passing? Think about sharing with someone you trust the answers to these and other questions which are important in your life, and jotting down what your plans for funeral. This could be written into your will, or included in an "final arrangement" document, which is intended to be used with your will. "Funeral Rituals and the Body Following the Death" which follows, can aid in determining your choices.

Are there any important duties that living people must accomplish once their needs have been resolved? We saw this in chapter 8 and 9 leaving the world without a complete resolution to business could slow our progress and can have a an adverse effect on family members and those who seek closure. In a practical terms, aids us to become an ancestor. Take the initiative of making contact with the most important people in your life, and in some manner with people who would benefit by hearing from you in the event that you're able to remember a few months, or even a couple of days of lucidity before your death. Writing letters are a great method of expressing your thoughts in the event that this is not possible.

even if you wish the letters read only at the time of your death or in the event that you need someone else to write them on your behalf. Numerous cultures suggest that we acknowledge and accept our mortality and be prepared to pass away at any time. Staying up to date with those around us is a crucial element of this preparation.

Other than skydiving Do you have some outstanding things that are on the "bucket list"--experiences that will inspire you to sing once you've achieved the other objectives? If yes then why not do all you can to turn them into real? While a few months of life will never substitute years of experience The soul is a living creature that can undergo rapid changes and changes. As we approach that threshold, our condition of our mind and heart will have a significant impact on the next steps Spending time doing things that help to energize the soul will help during the journey that is to come. When you've considered the things you'd like to be able to experience during your last months take a look at whether you are able to implement some of these plans and dreams right now, even if do not have any indication that you're dying.

The End of the Days

Would you like to do in the final week of your life if could have it to yourself however you want?
Do you prefer to stay inside or wake up early? Do you prefer to being at home in the natural surroundings, or in public, going to your most loved places? How important will solitude and contemplation be in your final days here on earth? Have you got a religious

practice that you'd like to give more time? If you don't are a spiritual person but you are attracted to a specific tradition. If so you can request a person who is a part of the tradition to join you on a ritual or ritual on behalf of you. Local pastors, as an instance could offer an oath ceremony at your residence, or an Buddhist teacher might impart wisdom about dealing with death, or an Lakota practitioner might offer the pipe (chanunpa) ceremony or an in-person purification ceremony (inipi) to clean the way in the honor of your passing. Requests to assist in dying are usually welcomed by the majority of religious leaders as well as communities. It is an opportunity to offer comfort to loved ones who live and those who are who are dying, and also an avenue of assistance for the soul during its transition to the next stage of its life and of course it is a valuable reward to those who offer it. People who are dying often choose to spend at least a part of their days prior to death , working on tasks and spending time with their loved family members. If you've experienced a turbulent and distant relationships, this is the time to apologize and share sensitive information that were difficult to share prior to the time of death. "Don't delay until dead to reveal what you think of their relationship," my dying grandmother told my mother. The less surprise stories (e.g., "I'm not your biological father"; "I'm not your biological father") the more pleasant.

The more you communicate in your dying times (e.g., "You have an older sister who you haven't met") and the more you'll be grateful for the company of relatives and friends. Becoming up to date on your life can also make room for any emotional bombs family members may drop on you, positively or negatively. If you are aware of this difficult part of ending your life, you'll be helping in ensuring a smooth funeral, a less difficult grieving process for those who live and a more smooth transition into the next phase of life.

Nothing stands in your way of the next life after the closing ceremonies and visits with loved ones are over. Are you able to recall a moment that you shifted your attention on the future before embarking on a big trip or life change in your mind, imagining what it might be like when you got there? Perhaps this is an act of comfort during moments of transition, putting some of us before time to be with us upon our arrival. It's normal to indulge in this kind of apprehension contemplation when you're planning to die. As if the dead are within the space, family members and family members who serve as the companions of those who are dying frequently recount the conversations between the ancestors and person who is nearing death.

"What happens after your body is gone?" is the most important issue. This is not for the general public and for you, but specifically for. Do you know what will happen to you in the moments or hours and days when your body is no longer working? Are you going to leave the planet in the near future? Do you think you'll go to heaven or another dimension, or even rebirth? Perhaps you'll discover a way to join with nature or the elements? Are there any spirit or force that are ready to assist you with the next steps? If you have strong convictions about the future will be able to see the way ahead. People who are a believer are more equipped to confront the change with confidence because they possess the foundation of faith to envision the portion of themselves that is moving ahead and explore the way. People who meditate or have an innate curiosity about being in the dark are likely to view the path of the soul that leads to death with curiosity instead of being scared. Do not let fear stop your from thinking about death, even though you don't hold any beliefs or practices of spirituality. Focus your attention to the future and invoke the spirit of courage and openness in your thoughts and your heart. Think about asking your ancestral guides and ancestors for permission to discuss details about the dying process , if you've tried the methods that are described in the book. If so consider it, please be considerate of yourself and let them know that you need to learn what you should know now. Be aware that even atheists who profess to be religious come back from near-death or temporary death to share stories of endless love, bliss and joyful reunions with their ancestors.

Chapter 13: Soul Personas

Reincarnation is believed to have many positive aspects. Our departure from this world is not the end of the world. We'll see those with whom we are close, are given more than one opportunity to meet again, etc.. But do we actually belong to those who have lived in the past and who will live the future lives? In what ways are we different in our lives, and in what ways do we share a commonality?

Identity as self-image

In the course of our lives We are sometimes ourselves Sometimes we're not, and at times we're not sure. The way we perceive ourselves is based of our thinking and emotions and physical condition and the other people around us, our conditions, and even our age. Sometimes, we can be irritable or calm. Sometimes, we can be a calming force. In one moment, we might declare, "I am happy. I am hungry.' In the next instant, I would like to quit. I'm exhausted.'

Our self-image can change dramatically. We thought we were unsteady but now we realize that we're adroit. We believed we were misunderstood as by the loners. But it appears that we're famous. We thought we had luck but then we discover that we've been hit with a some bad luck. It was thought that we're insecure with girls, but now we're aware that we're homosexual.

Saying "I" now is different from how we used to say it 10 years ago. Ten years from now,, we will be different. In the past, we were able to declare 'I'm insecure. I suffer from acne. I'm good at French. I don't have a boyfriend as of yet. I am in love with my dad.' In 10 years' time, we may say that "I'm divorced. I have two kids. I am very passionate about my job. I wear contact lenses. I've been in love with them again.'

144

Stage hypnotists can cause people to believe they are famous or chickens - or perhaps famous chickens. Our day-to-day identities as well as our self-image might have been replaced with seemingly hypnotic ideas from our peers and even ourselves. It is possible to talk about self-deceit or illusions, or in severe instances of megalomania or paranoia. Psychologists and psychiatrists are knowledgeable about identity issues (apart of their personal issues with identity). The old saying 'know yourself is a reference to the fact that our self-image is usually a source of mystifications. Our self-image also shifts depending on our experiences of either success or failure (a fundamental concept within Alfred Adler's Individual Psychology), with our feelings of happiness and discontent (a fundamental concept of Freudian psychoanalysis) and with the development of comprehension or confusion as well as our physical state.

145

The picture is much more complex. There are also different and sometimes contradictory identities simultaneously. Faust's lament, 'Zwei Seelen, ach, wohnen in meiner Brust!' ('Two souls, sadly are inside my heart! '), is the best illustration of this. The term "transactional analysis" refers to the Adult, the Parent as well as the Child within each of us as the three faces of our "I". As a parent, we are able to identify with those we consider to be our peers. When we are puberty, we can look up to others and compare our self with heroes, no matter if they are in the past, on the silver screen or even living in the next corner. in Play it Again, Sam, Woody Allen tries to be identified as Humphrey Bogart, and again we might be a part of Woody Allen.

The Jerusalem Hospital has specific admissions policy that is geared towards Christian tourists who are razed to find out they've previously been Jesus as well as

John the Baptist as well as for Jewish tourists who discover that they are King David. Now, there are past-life regressions that aid us in identifying with fascinating or fulfilling lives.

In addition to all these shifts, inner conflicts and connections with other people There is a vast part of us that we are not aware of and that's the subconscious. This is the subconscious's chapter or more accurately, a library within itself. It is possible that our lives are divide into different strands experiences with various subpersonalities. The first book to explore the syndrome of multiple personalities is Sybil (Schreiber 1973). To a certain extent, every person's personality is a collection composed of parts that are relatively separate. It is possible to be a shrewd businessperson while being an amiable and patient father and mother. Or the opposite. Psychotherapy utilizes this technique as a method of therapy in Ego

State Therapy (Watkins 1979; Edelstein 1981), as well as for Gestalt Therapy and Psychosynthesis.

Then we could experience an impairment in memory. A lot of people are unable to recall huge portions of their lives. We may not remember the instances when that we were angry or instances when we were subject to the scorn of others. Some of our experiences and personality are "underground". Subpersonalities are a result of loss of memory and become without control, we can be near psychosis. Our personalities are like an extended family, with members who may mix, merge or break off. We have insensitive and sensitive members, both younger and older ones, foolish wiseacres, unintentional copies of other people with black sheep, and criminals who rarely at home (at at least in the majority cases). The idea that a soul is an person, an unbreakable entity could be the case. It's

certainly valid for our bodies. The notion
that people are individual, unbreakable is
a fable.

Self-images that are pathological
A healthy self-image is created when our
subpersonalities coexist in a peaceful and
respectful family unit; when we adult,
parent and child simultaneously; and
when the male and female aspects of us
are in harmony (preferably males in the
leading role in the male body as well as a
woman with female form). Our self-image
is distorted when members of the family
do not get along or ignore one another
(for example , in cases like Sybil) as well as
when secluded identities enter the family
home. In the absence of obsession, we
could legally be considered to be insane,
and not accountable.

Many people believe that their higher self'
as their ideal self that can only show itself
in part. They are members of sects and
hold to high-minded worldviews. Their

idea of what humanity should be is to shed the human aspects and to become a type of angel. This to me is an the ultimate evolutionary overstretch. It's not about trying to be the person is you, rather instead who you imagine you ought to be. The angel image is an image of a shining robot that is a mechanical and insignificant attempt to transcend the realities of our world and ourselves. A successful identification can lead to inhuman machines, inaccessible peoplewho are smiling and giddy with self-pity, and adoring their own private heaven. Their own mortality is evident in the dark and suffocating environment for those who are not. Self-hypnosis is a way of seeing the world as the light of their lives. In the world of self-hypnosis, pain, sickness despair, doubt hopelessness, meanness, and despair are unreal or not present thoughts of the inactive soul. When self-delusion is lesser potent force, the outside world can be dangerous, filled with swindlers and False Jesuses (from various clubs) as well as cynics, blockheads and sleepwalkers. The outside world can be dark. The world is a risky and a bad place, hell. Through a weaker self-hypnosis, we need to recognize our flaws. We then become performers in the timeless melodrama "Oh, woe is me and I'm yearning for the angel inside our lives (or outside of us) and perpetually wrestling with the devil or beast in our lives. A look at the different human-like identities we can be assuming is provided in the table below.

If we believe that we belong to something that is superhuman, we disregard or suppress the subhuman the animal. The animal in us changes. People who are powerful and conscious for their weaker "lower" sub-personalities block their entry. There are people who battle with a wild animal that is part of them, in lieu of calming it down and transform it into a loyal and observant dog. The animal that was exorcized becomes an animal that is feared; the animal is a symbol or even it is even a pet. The desire to rise into darkness, the animal is sucked into darkness.

A prisoner in a concentration camp might naturally imagine his wife at to her home in heaven in the form of an angel. A victim of torture may be able to imagine the world as hell. Hells and heavens created by self are inherently pathological. Every kind of projection, shifts and reactions could occur. When we lived in Victorian times, young men could imagine beautiful girls and believe they could be beasts of the masturbation. It's not easy to live. That's what we learn to do as we age. The imperfection is the birthplace of the perfect, the eternal grows out of the temporary, peace coming from war, health and happiness out of illness, peace out of fear, and wisdom from the foolishness of. After depersonalization and inflation, other most significant identity disorders include depersonalization, derealization and what I'll refer to as 'deseparation'. Depersonalization refers to the loss of "I" but remaining conscious, but not feeling an identity or personality. The thought of 'being in the past' is not enough to provide the sensation of being there. We are empty bottles of thoughts that are fleeting and vivid shadows. The reverse is also true around. We are constantly being surrounded by, and entrapped in, a void of reality. All we see is decoration and cardboard. It's gray paste, and the bewildering, infuriating, totally absurd pretense that it's real. Jean-Paul Sartre calls it La Nausee. Solipsism, the idea of the belief that just "I" exists and the rest are mere reflections of my consciousness is the derealized intellectual dummy. Mysticism transcends the human self image by identifying to an object another individual and other living beings or with the landscape. It is possible to transcend the division between ourselves as well as the environment around us by dispersing ourselves over the globe, and becoming one with everyone (thus being one with God) and the mystic unity, the unio unity. The clinically speaking, this state resembles depersonalization , or derealization. In the first case, there is no longer a sense of our own reality. In the second state, we no longer feel the reality of another as well, and in the third state, we do not ever feel any distinction between us and others. A medical translation of unio mystica would be deseparation, the loss of distinction. The propagators of separation tend to join with the universe and with God or with all and rarely with their spouse, their neighbour, or even the cat that lives across the street. A tree , or another living thing or object, without the risk of reacting - or refusing to respond to their desire to be one is more suitable. In intimate human relationships occasions of healthy and valuable separation could occur. It is one among the most appealing aspects of sexual encounters, even though many people prefer to lose their own self than finding a new partner.

Our identity, the essence of who we are, the person we are the 'I' that we are, that is, therefore, not an unchangeable and inseparable fact and is instead the product of changing identification processes, susceptible to influence and arbitrariness. The process of identification is an inherent and fundamental feature of our conscious. It is a morphology that has its own as well as it's own pathology. When we depersonalize, our identification ceases and the result is an absence of identity however, our body and mind remain in place. Through the practice of depersonalization, our body awareness is the anchor for our self-image. We usually experience our bodies spatially and with our focus on our head, or behind our eyes.

Our diverse identity, the larger self and life plan , Crookall's work and his regression experience reveal that, after complete freedom from body and waking up in a healthy way it is possible to be free of insanity, confusion and defects However, we are not unalterable. Many dead who communicate with us acknowledge that they have done so, but forget the truth. People with discarnate feelings, who feel free and having easy access many sources of information, are often exuberant. Fully awake discarnates typically show themselves as being at their most effective in their incarnate state however, they are able to adapt to the subject as well as the people they encounter. In the immediate aftermath of death, many assume their appearance from the most recent time they felt well and then later, of stage of life and the state where they felt the most at their best. Later, some adopt a different appearance that is not tied to their past lives. They generally appear to others in the way that is at home with them. If they are interested in topics that were particularly important to them during a specific lifetime the person may assume the persona of that particular life. So, the self-image that comes from discarnate can be more flexible and solid than when they are incarnated. The individual's personality is unaffected.

People who are stuck in the twilight twilight etheric zone are able to indulge in their pet's emotions as well as pet thoughts and environments. They can also fall into their own dreams , often nightmares.

If we truly are our own person, we are an unfettered personal identity. Theosophists talk about"the Higher Self," however this implies a distinct self from our normal, or the lower. There are some who talk about'my higher self' and'my lower self'. As with'my self' these phrases are misleading since they indicate identity in terms of having something rather than actually being it.

The higher self is often portrayed as being all-knowing, all-wise and unchanging from the start to the conclusion of the existences. It is not the whole truth. Of course, there exists a continuity between entities. I will refer to this entity as the'soul' from now on. Christopher Bache (1990) first discusses the "oversoul," however, he later states that "soul" is the best name for our identity through all our lives and intermissions.

I refer to it as 'spirit' for all of the
phenomenon of consciousness, which
includes self-consciousness. The nature
and the structure of self-consciousness, or
the self-image, develops out of the
experiences we experience in our body.
Experiences that are physical, incarnate is
more extensive than discarnate, psychic
experience, leads to self-awareness and
awareness. The soul awakens and
concentrates on its various incarnations.
Once we become aware of our self the
soul can bloom in the state of discarnate.
It is through the body that we can be the
medium for spiritual awakening. The soul's
beginning state is consciousness due to
the body it is a part of, and following
death , it is unable to remember anything
(falling to sleep). As it ages, it begins to
dream even after death, and dreams grow
increasingly vivid and eventually the soul is
awakened by meeting others who are real
discarnate before becoming self-aware

159

and accountable.

In discarnate we're exactly like the person that we were at the peak of our life, except without physical limitations and with access to our various personality. The personalities from diverse lives are similar to the different subpersonalities that we encounter in the same life. In the event of our death and we are reincarnated, we carry on the character of our previous life, however, we soon get access to the past and, consequently following a review of our past lives, we develop into a larger persona that is usually focused on the most conscious and most mature life. The complete self is lost with every incarnation, and in sleeping state: there is a lapse in consciousness but not a change in our personality.

Chapter 14: Reincarnation Possible

The Christian religion, like most religions, affirms that we are immortal souls. Reincarnation affirms the same. Furthermore, reincarnation is a reality in this age, even though it's not a religion, but rather an academic thesis is based on the belief that religions are a form of faith in God and, as such they're all good. The distinction between Christianity and Reincarnation lies in Christianity believes that when we die , we will be taken to heaven or Hell for the rest of our lives, if we have performed good deeds and our conduct has been defined by the Ten Commandments announced by Moses or, on the other hand we've chosen to follow the path of eviland are harming the other. Reincarnation does not believe that souls are punished for the rest of their lives. Reincarnation believes in severe and painful punishments, but they are only for a short period of time. It is inconceivable to imagine that God as our father in love and who is a loving father to every one of his children, does not give us another chance to learn from our mistakes and access the heavens of happiness. We all have our own uniqueness and yet share a similar destiny. All of us will experience God's presence God and complete the task that God has given us in the eternal existence. Let's consider the case of one woman who had been deceived and transferred to another continent and then forced to drink drugs and prostitutes before becoming bitter and had negative emotions until her death. could be sent to hell. But did she really feel made to live a shabby life. Did she keep her confined to death? I'm sure not. It's more credible and based on the notion that we all lead several lives, including those we learn that if we hurt others we can rectify our mistakes and pay back the people we hurt, and also be aware why love is the way to the perfect. The punishments we are dealt are temporary, and we'll never be destined to endure all eternity. In a lot of cases, it is frequently mentioned as a criticism of the reincarnationprocess, the lack of explanations as to why there an increase in population, and , consequently the large number of souls who have been incarnated.

This criticism will also be applicable to Christianity and other religions since it is believed that the amount of souls who were born on earth from the time of the first human will be significantly greater according to Christianity and other religions, than is if you accept the idea of reincarnation. It is a belief that a lot of them have already come and are simply reliving their lives in a new way. Additionally, God has no difficulty and can use the flow of spirits, in creating the amount of souls that are required to carry out his purposes. The physician presents the beginning of the third chapter his work which includes a comprehensive explanation of how souls which are born from the energy of a huge mass. It also is a description of the care they provide for Mothers of Incubator , as they are able to strengthen. A lot of the moral rules and the spiritual rules that should be used as a guide for Christians and the followers from other faiths and religions, are like the ones that Reincarnation advocates and those that were revealed through the declarations of spirits within themselves, and communicated through mediums.

DIFFICULTIES IN ACCEPTING REINCARNATION

If reincarnation was studied as an issue of science it will be easier to comprehend and accept because research conducted across the five continents yield the same findings that lead to the same conclusions. But, since most of the population of the planet is a part of any of these religions which have deny the possibility of reincarnation, it is not believed in due to religious reasons. It doesn't matter what are the grounds that cause the belief that reincarnation is real, as there are always false beliefs about the reality. If you want to change the beliefs of someone, it is very difficult.

Furthermore, the scientific discoveries in the case of the reincarnation theory, have been criticized for a considerable amount of time before they are accepted by the vast majority of the world. The similar thing happened with the revelation that Earth being round, not flat as was believed to be.

When Copernic (1473-1543 a.C.) concluded that the earth as well as all planets were subject to two movements in translation and rotation around the sun. He then hid the original manuscript within the manuscript he resigned to research to avoid the religious opposition. Galileo (1564-1642 a.C.) was the founder of modern science, was a target of the Catholic Church for defending Copernicus's assertion that the earth revolves in the direction of the sun. He was only able to save his life when he reversed from his assertions. The scientific theory of the Earth's rotation around sun was contested for over two centuries and was later accepted by scientists around the world for a longer period of time before the population's world accepted it as to be valid. The Origin of Species , by Charles Darwin, published in 1859, laid the foundation for the development of species that continued until the time of the time of. According to his theory that we came from an ancestor who was similar to monkeys. The thesis seemed fanciful like the way resurrection of the soul is for us today but the discovery of fossils proved that there were beings that evolved at different times between the small monkey and man and this stunned the scientific community and, initially was resisted because it seemed too unbelievable. The major scientific discoveries that present as irrefutable evidence In many instances, they weren't accepted in their time, due to the fact that they clashed with the limiting knowledge and beliefs of the time.

In the present when you ask individuals from a common culture level whether they believe in the theory of atoms and particles of atomic nature, which according to the theories of the past they are the basis of what the world is composed out of of people would respond negatively.

SPIRITS ARE NON VISIBLE

The spirits are subject to completely different laws than those applicable to matter and need to be studied through the impacts. Although radio waves aren't invisible but we can recognize them due to their effects. Let's look at some evidence that prove that spirits exist. They appear frequently when they are summoned by mediums. They communicate and write to mediums. They do not appear until they've returned to earth, and have been become incarnated into a body. We've all heard of séances with spirits that have many participants. There are many people across the world who can are able to communicate with spirits and see them. In the United States there are many television shows that explore this phenomenon. The families of dead individuals who participate in these shows receiving messages and texts sent from their deceased acquaintances confirm this. The contents of the messages with information only the deceased person could have known suggest that the messages came from the deceased person. The television channels Infinite and A&E broadcast programs about psychic people who communicate with spirits of deceased people. Spirits have appeared in all times in a variety of ways, beginning in 1848 at Hydesville (New York) where spirits communicated with people in the Fox family and was able to answer any question with the sound of bangs which were clearly heard. Since the time, many famous personalities who speak to spirits have become famous as such, for example Chico Xavier and Divaldo Pereira in Brasil and Sylvia Browne in United States. True facts concerning spirits can be learned to people, with some cases they are recorded in video.

SPOONTANEOUS REMEMBERIES OF PREVIOUS LIFE

Many people from both the past and more recent times have experienced spontaneous memories, and have rekindled images clearly traced from their previous lives. In some instances, they've found evidence from the earlier life which confirm the fact that it exists. Doctor Brian Weiss explains us in his book Mirrors of Time, how one woman discovered the existence of her former life, without doubt:
A single of the more remarkable instances in the search for evidence that it is related to the name Jenny Cockel. As a young girl, she was haunted by memories of an earlier life in Ireland and in which she passed away while her children were very young. As an adult (she was reincarnated a few years following her demise) she decided to look for those children and discovered only five children of eight she was born with in that previous life. A lot of those who investigated the

possibility of reincarnation did not believe in her. In an instant, they were in a situation that stirred up their curiosity. As a result, they set out to research and test their patients, those who were influenced by regressions from previous lives to past lives. The result was where they realized that reincarnation actually existed. DIFFERENT TYPES OF REGRESSIONS Regressions can be classified into different types and can be classified into three categories that are: in the present as well as in past lives and in the Sky or Home Sky. Every day in the millions of cities across five continents psychologists, doctors psychics, specialists from the various fields of science, use hypnosis to bring back memories of earlier lives of patients who are seeking a solution to their fears, conflicts and physical ailments. While the majority of people don't believe in reincarnation, they share their stories about their previous lives and often believe that they have lived several lives prior to the one they're actually living. The reason for this is that those who control regressions want for the patient to travel to the point of death in the story they're talking about and examine at what happens to them following the death. They tell their an inner knowing that they will continue to live as spirits. Of course, they forget the fear of dying because they have now a conscience that they are immortal, and they are confident that the spirit of our soul returns back to earth, following some time of happiness and rest, in a new body, to carry on their studies and spiritual growth and perfection, as the spirits tell that they will in the regressions. It is well-known that the most effective methods of treatment for psychiatrists is to use the power of hypnosis to go back to childhood and childhood with the patients who are seeking traumas that caused them to have problems in adulthood. No one doubts the truths they reveal, but the stories of who are familiar with older people can provide be proof. The evidence isn't there to suggest in our subconscious, and I will affirm that our spirits will be able to withstand the rigors of regressions that occur in this life although it may be imagining when it comes to previous life regressions, even though that it is the same entity who tells the tales. I do not believe that God has provided us with brain-based mechanisms or even spiritual that can cause our minds to make mistakes, or even make us believe that we are using the same method of hypnosis. Doctor. Ian Stevenson is perhaps the only investigator to have the most number of documented instances of stories from recent years as well as non-recent stories, with some fully confirmed and some only partially in the files and records of famous people who's lives are in line with memories from their previous lives.

The doctor mentioned had 2000 cases stored in The computer system of the department of Parapsychology of the University of Virginia and it was the author of two intriguing books: Twenty Cases That suggests the Reincarnation, along with four books of, Some Reincarnation Cases. Numerous researchers have concentrated on engineering, the state of hypnosis, also known as trance. It is a state of mind that begins after death and is completed when you returning to Earth. The mid-life period is also known as Bardo or Bardo, also known as the Other Side, Home or Heaven. Home is also called Heaven. Heaven is the location or dimension that we originate from and then return every when we die. INVESTIGATORS DON'T BELIEVE REINCARNATION REINCARNATION While there are numerous instances of investigators who at first seemed to be absurd, we're only going to highlight three.

A psychiatrist with a high profile in the time he refused to believe in reincarnation Brian Weiss, is one of the most well-known examples. He was confronted by an astonishing fact and instantly began investigating the possibility of reincarnation. He and the two other researchers ended up not just accepting it and defending it, but doing so with excitement.

Dr. Joel H. Whitton doctor and author of Life between lives, stumbled, in the midst of the bard in between lives when he was aged 28 in 1974. He was devoted for a long time in guiding his patients back to earlier lives and never thought of investigating what happened to souls who was between the previous existence and another. We had already mentioned that this is a time for many things for spirits. Doctor Whitton was already leading Paula Cousidiene into the state of trance inside the same building that there was the Society of Psychic Investigation of Toronto was operating. He delved into past lives and was able to hear details about a previous life. Marta Paine, born in the ranch of Maryland 1822, made a decision to make clear certain aspects about her life. Prior to becoming Martha She made a mistake when she said "take me back to the time before becoming Martha" and hoped to travel back to her past life. As her instructions stated that she should go to the time prior to becoming Martha which is the space in between lives. She recounted the details of her experience as a spirit the realm of The Other Side: The sky is my view... I am able to see a farm and the rancher... It's dawn... and the boy... appears to be sleeping and the sun casts long shadows over the burnt field... with fields covered with trees. What's up at the top of the world? The hypnotizer asked the patient.

It is... I am waiting... until I am born... My eyes are watching what my mother is doing.

Is your mom still there? She's at the gas station , and... she is having issues... with how... in order to... to take her gas plunge. Why is she having issues? Since my body... it's too heavy on the girl... I'd like... I'd like... to remind her to be vigilant... both for herself also... in my case. What's your name? I do not have any name. Incredibly confused, Dr. Whitton gave to him over his ear the instructions to induce amnesia. He then took the patient back to the room with yellow walls and back to the year XXX.

Another surprise came from North American psychic Silvia Browne. When she helped a brand new client who wanted to lose weight using a psycho-hypnotic regression, she registered it part of the

Nirvana Foundation for Investigation; it was established and registered by the California State Department in 1974. California in 1974. When she was treating her client, she did not be concerned about reincarnation. She did not argue against it or deny it but she did say she had other things to do. She was giving classic hypnotherapy to a man when he began talking about his life in Egypt which he claimed to be the builder of pyramids. He explained complex and intriguing artifacts used to defeat gravity, including those that Dr. Browne could not comprehend. He then began to speak in an unintelligible language. Then, when the time he was awake, he started to speak in a normal manner. Doctor Browne presented the tape to a colleague from Stanford and requested him to find the the language that the patient spoke on the tape. The tape was scrutinized by experts in the field of languages and they concluded that the nonsense language the patient spoke of were a dialect of the VII century a.C. that was used by some builders of pyramids which were from the past of Egypt.

If the dialect was a product from the imagination and imaginings of the person it is unlikely that the person who was hypnotized matches their memory and descriptions of the processes they experienced while they were flying in the air.

From this we have found it clear that hypnosis can trigger relapses back to memories of our actual lives past lives, or the intermediary between the one and the next.

REGRESSIONS ARE PROOF OF REINCARNATION

Everyone who talks about past lives, even those who don't believe in Reincarnation, are of the opinion that we need to be kind and compassionate to one another and that we all have souls and body. the sense that we're here in this Earth to gain experiences, gain knowledge, and grow spiritually, and that the endure and relationships with people from different places are what let us grow and progress. It is also stated that when we die, view our body, we are looking at it from a height or level of a ceiling, as well as the surrounding space. The most amazing thing is the fact that regressions make us recall our lives in the past are remembered after death. when we are in an alternate dimension called Home The ones we have are amazing and extraordinary.

It is vital to note that in this realm, we don't have a physical body, which we have already left, therefore, we can't speak about the possibility of having recorded memories from the ADN.

Conclusion

When it comes down to death, you cannot say it's over. It's far from it. A couple thousand years of worth. It will all end eventually. However, your soul will feel like it has learnt everything it needs. You won't be able or ready to reincarnate after that point. You will become part of the astral reality and transcend your physical self. However, this can only occur after karma has completed its task.

Karma is a way of bringing about some harmony in the universe. There are many types of energies that surround us. Therefore, it is necessary to keep an order in the universe to avoid any kind of catastrophe. I have always believed in "You reap what You sow", and that is why I tried my best to live my life the right way. Everything that you do will eventually come back at you. Therefore, you must be mindful of what words and actions you choose.

There have always been misconceptions regarding karma. People will even say they don't have any obligation to offer their assistance because it's another person's karma. Consider it this way: our karma is formed by the karma that others have done. You may see someone in poverty now, who may not have done any good in his previous life. Similar to us, they may have believed that the karma must be left alone to work its magic while they enjoy their wealth. The person was reincarnated into a poor person, simply because they refused their help when offered. If you also believe in this belief, please answer the following question: Who do think will be the next victim of bad karma?

We don't simply live and then die. Our souls are made from pure energy. It is energy that does not simply vanish after the death of the physical bodies. Good things are necessary to sustain that soul's spiritual growth. This is why we learn all our lives and keep on learning through the Astral World. This is where we uncover all of our bad habits and learn how to fix them. We learn, improve and then start again.

Many people will argue that "since you don't remember, it doesn't add up" but that is wrong. It doesn't matter how long it is kept in the Akashic Books. All people subconsciously recall everything. The difference is that not all of it is conscious. Sometimes a memory could appear as a detour, a dream or even an intuitive feeling. We are not conscious of everything. Therefore, we cannot live or yearn to have a life other than our own.

We already know from deep within our hearts what we should do the moment we move into the next cycle.

9 781778 057960